AF400784

GORDON MATTA-CLARK
&
POPE.L

IMPOSSIBLE FAILURES

CLARION

GORDON MATTA-CLARK
&
POPE.L

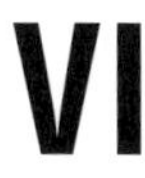

Dedicated to
Pope.L
(1955–2023)

Contents

Curator's Note: Never a Failed Attempt
Ebony L. Haynes

In his book *Hole Theory*, Pope.L writes, "[LACK IS WHERE IT'S AT]," which I have been thinking about from many angles for many years. The idea to pair Pope.L's work with Gordon Matta-Clark's started with the concept of holes and a genuine appreciation for their practices that circle the void.

In his work, Pope.L asks if anything can truly be a void—voluntarily or not, we fill in or make meaning, essentially negating the presence of absence. When I asked Pope.L to participate in this show, our early conversations were preoccupied by the absence of Matta-Clark himself. Pope.L continually challenged the idea of uniting two artists when one is present to make new work, to position or reposition existing work, to guide or weigh in on decisions, but the other is not. Pope.L began his artistic career in the mid-1970s and performed his *Times Square Crawl* the year of Matta-Clark's death, in 1978. There isn't, in a sense, a conclusion to this pairing—the conversation is open-ended, akin to the gaps the work engages.

In *Impossible Failures*, 52 Walker's sixth exhibition and first two-person show, Pope.L's *Failure Drawings*, which he makes on found materials while in transit, are joined with Matta-Clark's conceptual sketches, which he referred to as "impossible ideas." Mining architecture, language, institutions, scale, and perceptions of value, Pope.L's and Matta-Clark's work takes on various forms, encompassing performance, film, drawing, and architectural interventions, that are highly dependent on place and space. A major focus of Matta-Clark's work was making intentional cuts into existing architectural structures, holes or gaps that allow for looking in and out. So in the gallery space, we incised two holes in the walls, one that permitted visitors to peer into a space accessible only to staff, and another that allowed a visual exchange between inside and outside the gallery, with Matta-Clark's *Bingo X Ninths* projected on the wall where you entered and exited the space.

When creating such works, Matta-Clark first considered the location and context of the structure, prior to determining the intervention or work itself. This is particularly evident in Matta-Clark's writings included in this volume. Similarly, Pope.L often responds to the where before the what. Their dealings with space and place are improvisational, whimsical, constant, physical (taking chainsaws to load-bearing walls in the case of Matta-Clark, and with Pope.L, dragging his body across city streets). To this end, Pope.L created a site-specific installation, *Vigilance a.k.a. Dust Room*, for the exhibition. This room came from a proposal that Pope.L and I worked on together years ago, involving a kinetic arm with a giant pink eraser on its end that would circle around a room as if it were the minute hand on a clock, gradually rubbing out the walls, pink eraser dust falling to the floor. Modifying this idea in direct response to the gallery space, Pope.L created a stand-alone, contained room, lined with panels of reflective Plexiglas and lit inside with an ominous blue wash. The fillings from beanbag chairs served as the "dust," activated by the movement of air pushed through the accordion vents outside the box. When you walked into the gallery space, you could hear the low din emanating from the room, sometimes feeling the vibrations of it through the floorboards, but you could see the storm-like trajectory of the air in the room only by peering through two small apertures in the wall.

In my conversation with Pope.L and Hamza Walker, we discuss the artists' embrace of the relationship between failure and hope, which ultimately brings us to the impossibility of failure, opening us to possibilities that come from working within and against extant structures and welcoming the unknown.

Failin' Good
Ebony L. Haynes, Pope.L, and Hamza Walker in Conversation

For this volume of Clarion, *I invited Pope.L and Hamza Walker to participate in a conversation around the liberating potential of failing and of creating an effect with both the material (the body, architecture) and the immaterial (the void, the meeting point of presence and absence). Pope.L mentions over the course of our discussion "the company you keep," and I am lucky to keep company with these two thinkers. Walker's work as a curator and writer is particularly relevant in discussing the pairing of Pope.L's and Gordon Matta-Clark's work. He looks at whether art "functions critically" in terms of how we live in the present, especially as it relates to space and architecture. In a way, it was an impossible failure to have Matta-Clark's voice in our conversation, and while texts he wrote in the 1970s follow these pages, I believe his ideas and questions are folded into our conversation to the point where it felt like he was in the room all along.*

EBONY L. HAYNES: I wanted to chat with you both about the wonderful show I was privileged to work on with Pope.L and the aura of Gordon Matta-Clark. When I was thinking about this conversation, I became especially interested in starting with the word "failure." Failure is a theme, a feeling, in the show, and in early curatorial conversations with Pope.L, we questioned what failure is and what it means to have something fail—the gap between the intention and the end result, the effect.

POPE.L: I've always been a little suspect of that term in the art world because—well, because the people typically involved in the art world come from a culture that is not one of failure. And black people have seemed to be failing for many, many years. Not of their own intention, obviously. I can get ignorance—you don't know something, or you can't know something. But failure? It was weird when I first started hearing this term thrown around. Why would anyone be interested in failure? But I realized some people are; they maybe think they are inoculated from failure. I guess I was intimidated by it. It's something I've been avoiding all my life. Why would I want to deal with this shit? I mean, I'm already dealing with this shit. Why would I want to make it into an academic kind of thing? You know what I'm saying?

HAMZA WALKER: A rational pursuit!

PL: Why would I put my head in the lion's mouth? That's an honest thought. Or looking at African peoples who come to the United States and who say they're not black, having their own issues with defining themselves, and I say, Yeah sure, for them maybe it's a different deal. When you're failing for centuries, that's one thing, and then there are those who come in and the US represents a kind of nonfailure. Like, Gordon is second generation—his father was from Chile.

HW: Right, but that's a very intense conversation, actually.

PL: Fuck yeah.

HW: It's interesting that you would come in on that note, thinking about those who have immigrated to the United States—from Africa or the Caribbean—and an identification of being black in a country that is seen as a place to succeed; and then within that narrative of the country as a place to succeed, what African Americans might represent in terms of failure: Don't be that. It is a very complex foil that African Americans have played in relationship to other immigrants of African descent, from Africa and the Caribbean. And New York in particular is such a cauldron, where those things are very complicated to untangle.

PL: But, when I think of Gordon and failure, I don't think of it that way.

HW: Well, can I take a step back? Because I do see Gordon Matta-Clark as engaged with failure. Maybe we can try to square the term in some respects. What's interesting to me is that your lives, your careers overlap. I'm thinking of Gordon coming from Ithaca down to New York and being tight with Willoughby Sharp. One of his first exhibited pieces, called *Museum*, was at Bykert Gallery in 1970. And there might be the issue of failure around it, but I also think of it as being about the abject. And if one were to switch out the names and say it was a Gordon

Matta-Clark–Pope.L collaboration, I would believe it. That's based not just on the look of the piece but also on its list of materials: agar, water, dextrose, tryptone, glycerol, sperm oil, sodium chloride (and it's given in its chemical designation, NaCl), sugar, PET milk, V-8, cranberry juice, corn oil, yeast, chocolate Yoo-hoo—

ELH: That's a Pope.L word!

HW: —chicken broth, the hardware, gold leaf, local vines, galvanized pans, screw hooks, thumbtacks, Black Magic plastic sheet, known strains of *Mucor racemosus*, *Rhizopus apotheosis*, *Aspergillus niger*, *Penicillium notatum*, and *Streptomyces griseus*. So I was curious about the overlap in terms of the time frame: Gordon dies in 1978. Pope.L, you're at Pratt in 1973, somewhere in there, and then you finish your BA at Montclair State in 1978. And this is the rudimentary question—did you have knowledge of Gordon Matta-Clark at that time?

PL: Let's see. Yeah, in a way. The last two years of undergraduate school I read every *Artforum* published over a five-year period. I had decided that I just needed to teach myself. So sometimes instead of going to classes, I would just read these things and I probably ran across his stuff. But I remember at a later point I was reading his stuff, and I became more enlightened and asked, "What is it?" He wasn't very verbal. So unlike someone like Robert Morris or like Richard Serra even, some of those people who were writing at the time, it was hard to grasp what Gordon was about. He wasn't self-promoting as much, which I think was interesting about his whole thing. He didn't put a lot of text behind the image. That was my impression.

HW: The reason I ask this question about the overlap is because I see the two of you as the children of failure in a much grander sense. Meaning, when we think about the pillars of modernism as being urbanization, industrialization in the early part of the twentieth century as something to be celebrated, in connection to where they were by 1970 in New York City, you've got something that's much more like: Is this modernism in ruins? Gordon was growing up—and you, too, in a certain respect—in urban blight. Think about what cities were over the course of the sixties and into the seventies: an exodus for any number of reasons, an example of failure writ large. I think of the two of you as children of that failure, which is not in any sense a value judgment, but as a fact of life. And that's the starting point—the well—that the two of you would draw from. And there are different facets, aspects in that well for either of you, but it's still the same well, and that, I would argue, is what makes this show incredibly incisive, Ebony. The more I look at it, the more I look at the work in the show, outside the show, what those parallels are, it's quite amazing.

I'm wondering if you could talk a little about the scent, the feel, the texture of that period, that moment, the seventies, cities, socially, post–civil rights. The revolution is not going to happen! What are we going to do?

PL: Well, I would say this. I was supposed to go to Vietnam. My birthday was coming up and I thought I had to make a decision about either going to Canada or leaving the country to go to war. In fact, my mom told me, "If you don't go to school, you need to join the military like your uncles."

HW: And this would have been 1973, right? When you turned eighteen?

PL: Yeah. But luckily, Nixon withdrew in March. So the pressure was off of that. But that was what was on my mind at that time.

HW: Right. That kind of failure, politically, in terms of foreign policy.

PL: Yeah, definitely—

HW: And then just around the corner is Watergate.

PL: Yeah, but we don't know that yet. The Left felt at that time, because we withdrew, that they

won. But that was the big failure at the time for me—our failure in Vietnam was the first visible crack in this idea that America always wins. Despite what happened in Korea—which was a previous failure—but it wasn't as known, I guess.

HW: Right, and it's more complicated what the goals were, in a sense, and it's more of a marker of the Cold War, containment, the roll back of Communism to the borders of Russia. So, it has a different valence to it.

PL: I think that period allowed me to think more about domestic issues, like homelessness and about the relations of self to country. If I had to focus more on the issue of going to war, I would not, I think, have been allowed that kind of, maybe we could call it "leisure." It would have been about survival; and instead of survival in a foreign context, it was about survival in a domestic context.

ELH: In that sense, too, failure is not quite just something not succeeding, but being anti or counter to another sort of expectation.

PL: The more I think about this, is this just a product of something manufactured? Failure is not a problem. People fail all the time.

ELH: I don't think it is a problem. In some people's minds, installations like Gordon's *Museum* or Pope.L's *Black Factory* are not aligned with the traditional idea of how things can get acquired by institutions or collectors, in terms of their makeup or materiality. How do we place this in a museum? How do we archive it? "I don't understand how to make sure the Yoo-hoo . . ." They might be seen as a failure as a result. And while they're not failures, they are against what is considered good or accepted or successful, again depending on the definition. And "anti" makes me think of this prefix of Gordon's, the "anarch." Not just anarchy in his "anarchitect," but the anarch-ness of rethinking something, going inside it and rejigging it.

HW: In terms of the sociopolitical, cultural context in which Pope.L and Gordon were working and coming into maturity as artists, in terms of the avant-garde's bag of tricks, modernism was undergoing a critique and rigorous questioning, though within a kind of optimism. So by the time we get to it in the seventies, in some sense, one could read the times have actually caught up to the art.

And to what you were just noting, Ebony, I would say that there's a fallout at least at the level of medium. So painting, sculpture, a kind of medium specificity, had run its course. But Pope.L's and Gordon's work is hopelessly interdisciplinary. For Gordon, he's coming out of the discipline of architecture, being against or working off the discipline in which he was trained. Pope.L, for you I see the issue of interdisciplinarity as an amalgam of literature, theater, and performance. What about that interdisciplinary nature of the seventies? What about that is part of, perhaps, failure? Is it antiheroic?

PL: Yeah. I would say that—

ELH: Depending on who you're talking to, though, I mean it's heroic to many, also.

PL: But you don't know how it will play out. You may say, Okay, if I play the failure card as a heroic act or antiheroic act, then there's that. But I wasn't conscious of it in that way. I just knew that, at the time, you have what you have, and you decide, in a way, what you have. You can say, Well, I only have oil paint and I can afford oil paint. Or you can imagine a case where someone realizes, I can't afford that, but I want to be an artist. What can I afford? What is endemic to me?

ELH: The reason I wanted to title the show *Impossible Failures*, merging the concepts of the *Failure Drawings* and Gordon's "impossible ideas," is that I personally don't believe in failure. And if we're talking about the art world, failure really is impossible. Even if we're quantifying it in the sense of something not succeeding or not reaching some sort of expectation, I don't believe

that something can fail—there's so much room for hope and possibility when you work outside certain boundaries or traditions or ideals. And I think both Pope.L's and Gordon's practices are exemplary of that, in that they both push and rejig ideas, from all sides, of how one can make artwork, ultimately questioning what an artwork is, how you acquire it, archive it, document it, write about it, whether you should write about it. You're demanding the viewer to also be a steward of the work.

I wrote down this quote from Gordon, from a 1974 interview with Liza Béar, where he says, "Our thinking about anarchitecture was more elusive than doing pieces that would demonstrate an alternate attitude to buildings, or, rather, to the attitudes that determine containerization of usable space.…We were thinking more about metaphoric voids, gaps, left-over spaces, places that were not developed." He was interested in spaces on a "functional level that was so absurd as to ridicule the idea of function." We see him working out these impossible ideas in writing, too, such as in his manuscript for *Endless City*, a proposal for Anarchitecture, which starts, "Etc. And shred a city. A direct and non productive response to form following function" (pp. 13–14).

One thing I knew with relation to Pope.L in some capacity is that the 52 Walker staff would have to be prepared to work. Not just to put the show up but throughout the duration of the show, because this piece is alive. The installation is alive and requires our care and attention. Your *Fountain* works, for example, ask people to show care and refill water. And Gordon's work involves a similar type of interaction. It's almost as if you both break the fourth wall, and especially if we're talking about your theater practice, Pope.L. There's such an engagement with the people who are experiencing the artwork, from all angles of what that could mean. There's a requirement of that person.

PL: Well, back to what I said before, I realized, at one point, that, yeah, I can't afford paint but there's material that I can afford, and failure is one of them.

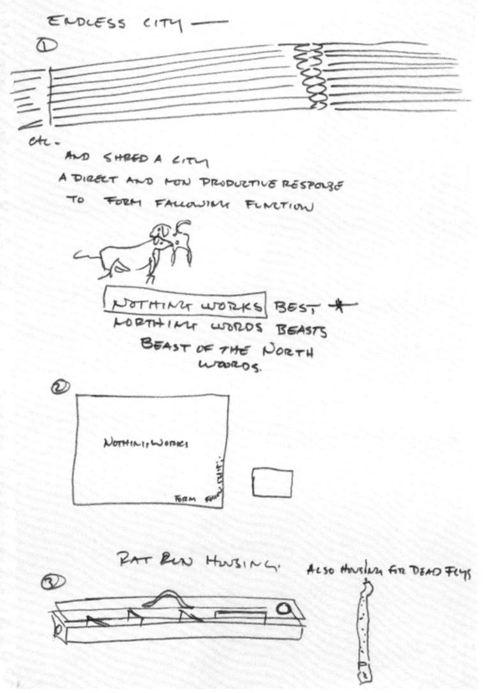

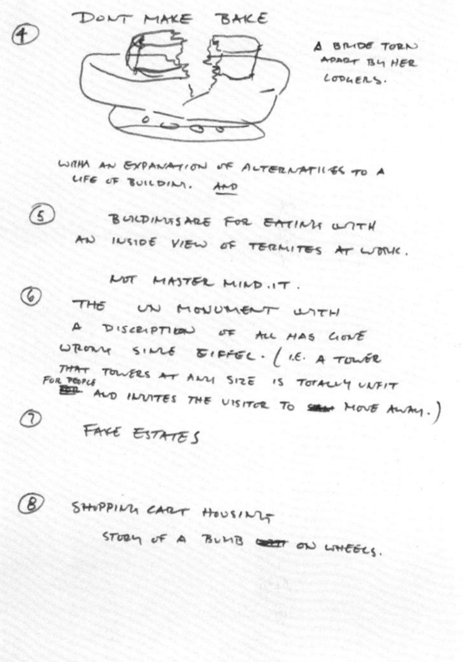

Pages 13–14
Gordon Matta-Clark, pages from *Endless City*,
a proposal for Anarchitecture, 1974

(9)

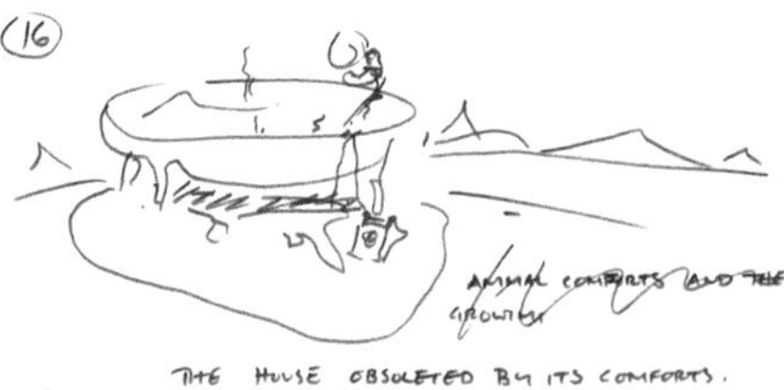

PAPER BAG PRIVACY

AN INVESTGATION OF THE
NATURE OF PRIVACY

COMPLETE WITH VOYERIST
SNAP SHOTS   UNDER SUB HEADING
SPACE TO LET YOUR EYES WANDER
THROUGH.
COLLECT ALL THE BOTTLES STILL IN PAPER BAGS
THAT CAN BE FOUND FROM HOUSTON TO RIVINGTON ON THE BOWERY.

(10)
THE COLLISION BETWEEN A
HOUSE MOVING OPERATION AND A
BRIDGE.   CAN DISPLAY AN ACCIDENT
REPORT OF HOW THE ACCIDENT HAPPENED
AND WHO WHAT WHERE .. FROM NY STATE
MOTOR VICHECLE BUREAU.

(11)   THE PERFECT STRUCTURE.

ERASE TO A NEW HORIZON

(12)   HELP RESOLVE OUR GAS-ENERGY-SHORTAGE
SHORTAGE OF GASOLINE ENERGY
BURN A NEIGHBORS HOUSE.

(16)

ANIMAL COMFORTS AND THE
GROWTH

THE HOUSE OBSOLETED BY ITS COMFORTS.

(17.)   SPACE TRAVEL

(18.)   A PERFECTLY COMFORTABLE SPACE TO
LIVE BETWEEN THE BRICK STONES
CORWALL WALLS

(19)   THE KIND OF LIVING YOU CAN CARRY ALONG.

SAME PROBLEM
NEW POSITION

HW: Didn't you once say that one of your favorite materials was lack?

PL: Yeah.

ELH: Talking about lack, one of your and Gordon's favorite materials is holes. You both love the void and the possibilities that open from it.

PL: Well, if you're going based off what Hamza said at one point about the toolmaker, how far can you go with that exercise? What can be a tool? I think it's a limit of your, call it what you want, imagination, tool-making ability, storytelling ability—all these things can be instrumentalized (maybe that's the term?) to amend. It doesn't have to be something physically you can hold in your hand. If anything stuck with me that I learned from those white people in the seventies who were calling themselves conceptualists is that this does not have to be a physical thing. You can take something that has no body and create an effect. And this is to a people who have been taught that they're just bodies for centuries.

HW: Right.

PL: They're saying that you can take something that has no body and create effects with it. What is that? What does that mean?

HW: Did that then inform, as I suspect it would, the primacy of performance for you?

PL: No, I mean it was more about a philosophical position in a way.

HW: I'm just thinking about the two things working in tandem. On the one hand, there's a kind of consciousness, it sounds like. Light bulbs are going on: What are they doing? Or this is the thing. But then what it does is shine light on or make one hyperconscious of the body. At that moment, certainly by the late seventies, performance as anti-illusionistic, using the actual body, was available to you as a practice. I'm just wondering how you squared that with the revelation about "the conceptual"?

PL: I think I just saw an opportunity there, and I was surprised that you could do this. I know you could do it in philosophy. I was pretty clear on that. But in art, I wasn't so clear that you could make a case for a material involvement in the immaterial. And that it could have an impact—according to how you deployed it, of course. The way these people did it was really kind of funny; they'd always do it in such an insular way. It was about linguistics and all this shit, and that was of interest to me. I was a nerd about that, sure. But I also thought, What are they not talking about? They're not talking about eating. They're not talking about surviving, where they're going to sleep at night. They're not talking about that shit. And I thought, Why? Or can you apply this immaterial thing to higher stakes? What I think are higher stakes, something like people being in pain.

ELH: I'm going to bring it to another place right now. What were your initial thoughts on the invitation of your being in a show with Gordon? What did that spark?

PL: Well, it was you asking me, right? It's like this conversation we're having, we asked Hamza to be here. It's the company you keep, you know?

ELH: Right.

PL: So at first it was that. Of course I'm going to initially say yes, because of the enthusiasm behind the people. So I wasn't very critical.

ELH: Were you worried about failure? Were you worried that something wouldn't work?

PL: Well, you know, when I thought about it after I hung up the phone, I said, Well, he's dead. What the fuck did I just say yes to? What am I getting involved in, you know?

HW: To do shows of this nature—

PL: You don't see many of them, for good reason.

HW: You know, when certain artists who I really admire pass away, I often say their work is still here and active and urgent. That's a technicality. It's as if they're still going, because the work is still radioactive. It's still transmitting. And that's how I feel about Gordon's work. He's a very interesting figure. A consummate, I would say, postmodernist, and I mean that in a particular kind of way. A post-minimalist artist. In terms of dates, he falls at the right time and moment. His drawings are where I find his chops on a formal level really come out—that arena is just absolutely amazing. Back to the interdisciplinarity. So what about that? What about you and drawing, Pope.L? The *Skin Set* drawings are the ones that obviously dominate when I think about you and drawing, but I wasn't aware of the *Failure Drawings* as a series, I guess.

PL: Well, I think I drew before I could write, as most kids do. It's so core. But it doesn't mean that you don't have a language supporting that drawing. You just don't know how to turn it into written phrases. Seeing the connection between the hand articulation we call drawing and the hand articulation we call writing was very key for me. Most of us were taught to do it—drawing—and then lose it, because we have more adult stuff to do as we grow up. But then, you know, becoming an artist, I started asking, What is the relationship between when you draw something and when you write something? Is there a difference? I think that question was important for me. I think most people would say, in terms of that writing-drawing question, that writing is functional, drawing is not. Now if you become an artist, then maybe the equation can shift. Drawing can become more communicative and more functional. But in fact, they're very close in terms of the articulation of your digits, of your hand, and of the way you think. Drawing allows me to basically create a wafer set where you're actually thinking through this image.

ELH: I have to say, that's really what I interpreted from the *Failure Drawings* linked with the "impossible ideas," the Anarchitecture drawings: they both emit this sense of ideating. It's free writing, but with drawing.

PL: Right. When I'm in meetings with my students, I will always draw for them. There are all these students who have my drawings in their notebooks, because we'll get to a point where I go, Okay, I have to make you a picture because I can't explain this to you. Even in logic, in philosophy, some of the most famous ideas have a picture. Lacan has his famous picture. Freud has a famous picture. Wittgenstein has a famous picture. We're always trying to match the writing with our imaging, somehow make them coalesce, reconcile them. It's a very childish thing to do, in a way, but that doesn't mean it doesn't have meaning or purpose or function, right?

ELH: It's interesting that you've used the word "childish" a few times in talking about drawing. Some of your drawings and Gordon's drawings are fantastical or, some might say, childish ideas. Like Gordon's *Energy Trees*, which propose a city in a tree, or the drawings that illustrate a system of transportation with hot-air balloons. In one of your *Failure Drawings*, there is this idea that a rocket would create a crater that is actually not large at all. And because it's in the form of a drawing, it's not considered as serious. And to what you said about writing versus drawing, if you were to write about or describe a transportation system that uses hot-air balloons, or define the engineering behind a tree city, it might appear more serious than it does when looking at watercolors or gouache flowing on paper.

HW: I mean, you can go back to Leonardo, right? The hot-air-balloon flying machines in drawings. And as fantastical, in some senses, as they sound, he was thinking through mechanisms from an engineering standpoint, which is interesting in connection to Gordon and architecture. Thinking about the role of drawing for architects, it can come down to the issue of function. Matta-Clark's sculptural paper works, the cuts, are in their own category, perhaps. But his drawings feel more fanciful and playful; they don't necessarily portray an architect's background.

ELH: Pope.L, do you think a lot about architecture? Is it of interest to you, personally?

PL: No. I find it a little weird that I say no, though, because in high school, I took four years of mechanical drawing with an architect. I thought that by doing this, I might be able to get a gig in architecture. But my teacher told me my math was too weak. I wish she had told me that two years before. In high school, it was the only class—even separate from art class, where you had to do other shit—where you could draw. And you had to draw with discipline, and you had to think about it within a system.

ELH: Are you interested in architecture, though, in terms of how it relates to people and movement in space?

PL: Maybe I have a willful ignorance. I meet people who talk about different architectural styles, and I wonder how they could think that way. They're so fly-by-night to me. I don't care what the history of that building is. I want to know if it's a place to be warm. I want to know that kind of stuff.

ELH: That's what I mean by how it relates to people or how people relate to it in space. What is architecture, practically? What is the purpose of the space or how is it being used? I'm steering the conversation in this direction because I see this as a connection between you and Gordon.

PL: I think he was able to see outside the building. Otherwise, I don't think he would have been able to draw into it, if you want to call his cuts "drawing."

ELH: Do you think you were seeing inside the building? Who is seeing in versus out through this hole?

PL: I can answer it in this way. My mom is an architecture. Wherever we would go, whenever we would move, it would feel like the same home. That's quite a feat. Now one of the big things about that was her book collection. Everywhere we went, we had to deal with this bookcase, which would dominate the house. In fact, I'm sure it probably influenced where we moved. "Well, we can't move here because I can't put my bookcase." The fact that she was allowing herself to think this way, when she had four kids and hardly any money, is interesting in that it is not the obvious, practical decision. But that bookcase and those books were there most of my life.

HW: Just hearing you talk about this all, it's a beautiful line of flight. When did you own your first home? And was that a psychological shift for you?

PL: When? What do you mean, "when"?

HW: Homeownership.

PL: You act like I do now. What kind of question is that?

ELH: Hamza, you failed!

HW: Oh, right. Well, I asked that, because the condition you're talking about is being a renter, moving from place to place. So where or when does one begin to think about architecture in terms of ownership?

PL: I think you have to have enough stability in your life to be able to step outside the structure. You've got to be able to set up a structure of thinking. There is the renter mentality. And it sounds so obvious that someone would think that way, but I can see it more now that I am actually buying a condo. It's a condo, though. I don't trust houses!

HW: Oh, I like that: the issue of land versus an interior.

PL: I think the issue is a lack of imagination on my part.

HW: But we know what lack means to you!

PL: People who own their condo will rent it to someone else. Maybe these people who rent don't feel the same way about their domicile that the owner does. As a renter you might not feel that connection or protect or use the space in the same way. I lived that way, physically and mentally, for a long time. I get it.

ELH: This is exactly the kind of conversation I was hoping to have, touching on space and physical interactions within it, whether it's within the void or physical and inhabitable, whether slicing through some sort of barrier between inside and outside. Documentation is everything, and here we have documentation of our failed conversation.

HW: Hardly a failed conversation! A conversation on failure!

PL: I think we laughed too much for it to be a failure.

Writings
Gordon Matta-Clark

Completion through Removal
n.d.

Completion through removal. Abstraction of surfaces. Not-building, not-to-rebuild, not-built-space. Creating spatial complexity reading new openings against old surfaces. Light admitted into space or beyond surfaces that are cut. Breaking and entering. Approaching structural collapse / separating the parts at the point of collapse.

Translating the diagram into its structural context. What's beyond the building's surface.

Rather than using language, using walls.

Looking through the thing. The ambiguity, what's there and not, as much not as the whole.

Usurpable void's. What happens when weight's. Release and working contained energy.

*

The meeting point released: spatial intersection where things are layered or suspended.

A cut that took three days and six inches of rain. Simple gestures.

Spatial complexities and admitting new light.

Edges
n.d.—1971

City edges ——————— Rather than finding more ways of using and exploiting what is left forgotten and remains empty it would be far more useful to allow dead ends their peace and quiet. If the cities use-pattern dwindles off to places seemingly forgotten except for each of us who finds it enjoying a short escape from total development, why rush back and insist it be altered to accommodate all—the failing of the architectural stage set mentality is its homogeneous accessibility to all and an oppressive mania for influencing the entire fabric in all its details over all its surfaces. Nothing's left alone. The professional devotion to care and responsibility leaves no space untreated, no surface uncovered whose final effect is a lifeless emptiness completely opposite to the emptiness at the end of the road or at the top of the stairs or at any point of non-use.

Beyond the wrong thinking of promoting more use, more total coverage in a city edges project there is also a highly simplistic view of the edges—again the issue is exploiting undeveloped areas. Therefore, rooftops, water fronts, empty lots, whatever known usable surfaces that are doing alright on their own are the target for "improvement." Due to that logic a whole range of obvious additions goes unseen, misunderstood and un-enjoyed if it can't be built on or worked with.

1.) Space between the edge of one building. Ones opposite and to all sides.

2.) The edges made by functional limits where services break through or reenter the ground i.e. Plumbing sewerage.

3.) Where the land also rises. Places where the natural or possible nature of the original land mass break through an excavated paved and superimposed system.

4.) Curb cuts—Gutters—Road and parking spaces.

5.) Pigeons, rat city, "paricites" Again the edge which is clearly derived in the city edges project is the underground for all its service and life—waste involvement. Its support of vital energy communication and disposal need is only part of how it functions as a home for our most familiar neighbors. The non-paying parasitic tenants and ultra—echo we squash, trap poison and gas.

Untitled Statement on *Bingo*
n.d.—1974

"BINGO" is the finalized title for a work that, in progress, was called "Been-Gone by Ninth." The piece involved the use of a "typical" American small-town home that was to be demolished for urban-renewal. The project began with a wonderfully adept telephone call by Director Dale McConathy to the Niagara Falls Planning Commission, through whom I was permitted to have free use of 349 Erie Avenue, a red-shingle house still in perfect condition.

Under contract with the city, I was to complete my work in ten days, during which time a major part of the exterior was to be sectioned into nine equal parts, measuring 5×9 feet. Eight of these facade segments were cut free, lowered intact and crated for transport to Artpark, leaving the center of the nine-part-grid undisturbed.

During the allotted working period the pace was a succession of ten and twelve hour days, non-stop, and at times involving as many as five other workers. The measuring, cutting and removing of the wall sections was continued right up to the hour the demolition crew arrived to tear down the house. The project was completed only because the workers called off the demolition until the next morning in order to allow me to safely remove the last pieces.

In keeping with a history of construction debris on the Artpark site, five of the eight crates were judiciously dumped, and with the forces of natural reclamation these building parts became evermore mysterious remnants in an elaborate celebration of abandonment.

So for the future, one of my goals is to delay the loss of the actual spatial experience and structural alterations by working in buildings where demolition could either be forestalled or be commissioned for occupied space. I shall also be focusing my attention on both ends of the scale: larger buildings and more specific structural details. While I shall be constantly interested in dealing more with structure-spatial situations typical to a variety of American and non-American regions.

The financing of these projects has been both private and state funded, running from under a thousand dollars to just over two-thousand. The better part of these moneys went both to my living and travel expenses while doing the work and my assistants' labor. Other expenses were photographic and film material equipment, rental and in one case, a two-week liability policy. I was not paid any commissions.

Locating the building is often less of a problem than might be thought, especially out of New York City in blighted urban industrial areas or where any kind of renewal is taking place. But as I have mentioned, both occupied and exhibition space are also possible.

Second Untitled Statement on *Bingo*
n.d.—1974

The earliest cutout works were discrete chunks of buildings taken from abandoned tenements left open to derelicts and stray dogs and to me. In these pieces, I was dealing with a non-acceptance of the space as defined by its given architectural limits.

A year-and-a-half ago, I set up a show in Genoa when without prior introduction an engineer became so intrigued with work in my portfolio that he gave me his old drafting studio to experiment with. As in the first pieces, I started by redefining the interior divisions; but as I was working in a heavy industrial area with some cranes available, the project grew to encompass the whole building.

Since then two other works have been realized more clearly emphasizing a unified treatment of the structural entirety of the building. "Splitting" was made possible by the enthusiastic support of Mr. & Mrs. Horace Solomon. This house was "undone" over a period of six-weeks in a New Jersey suburb with the help of one or two assistants and no equipment more sophisticated than Rockwell power hand tools. Besides its gestural clarity when seen from outside, the building was left standing long enough for visitors to experience the encompassing spatial complexity of the interior.

At the invitation of state funded "Art-Park" near Niagara Falls, New York and the help of Dale McConathy, I set up a building alteration called "Bing-go. Ne by nineth and days." This project involved laying out a grid of three horizontals, three vertical divisions of the main facade. The work was completed in ten days using a crew of five or six men cutting, removing intact, crating and the haulage of eight 7' by 9' half-ton sections of facade. At five PM just before the last section 8/9 was freed and crated, the bulldozer arrived. At seven the next morning demolition began reducing the building to splinters and powder in thirty-five minutes. The speed of these events prevented me from completing a final treatment of the work uniting north and south facades by removing a section equal and opposite from the remaining on the stripped side.

Gordon Matta-Clark's Building Dissections
n.d.

"By undoing a building there are many aspects of the social conditions against which I am gesturing. First, to open a state of enclosure which had been preconditioned not only by physical necessity but by the industry that profligates suburban and urban boxes as a context for insuring a passive, isolated consumer—a virtually captive audience. The fact that some of the buildings I have dealt with are in black ghettos reinforces some of this thinking, although I would not make a total distinction between the imprisonment of the poor and the remarkably subtle self-containerization of higher socio-economic neighborhoods. The question is a reaction to an ever less viable state of privacy, private property, and isolation."

"I seek typical structures which have certain kinds of historical and cultural identities. But the kind of identity for which I am looking has to have a recognizable social form. One of my concerns here is with the Non.u.mental, that is, an expression of the commonplace that might counter the grandeur and pomp of architectural structures and their self-glorifying clients."

"I have chosen not isolation from the social conditions, but to deal directly with social conditions whether by physical implication, as in most of my building works, or through more direct community involvement, which is how I want to see the work develop in the future."

"The act of cutting through from one space to another produces a certain complexity involving depth perception. Aspects of stratification probably interest me more than the unexpected views which are generated by the removals—not the surface, but the thin edge, the severed surface that reveals the autobiographical process of its making. There is a kind of complexity which comes from taking an otherwise completely normal, conventional, albeit anonymous situation and redefining it, retranslating it into overlapping and multiple readings of conditions past and present. Each building generates its own unique situation."

"I feel my work intimately linked with the process as a form of theater in which both the working activity and the structural changes to and within the building are the performance. I also include a free interpretation of movement as gesture, both metaphoric, sculptural, and social into my sense of theater, with only the most incidental audience—an ongoing act for the passer-by just as the construction site provides a stage for busy pedestrians in transit. So my working has a similar effect. People are fascinated by space-giving activity. I am sure that it is a fascination with the underground that most captures the imagination of the random audience; people can't resist contemplating the foundations of a new construction site. So in a reverse manner, the openings I have made stop the viewer with their careful revealings.

Moreover, I see the work as a special stage in perpetual metamorphosis, a model for peoples' constant action on space as much as in the space that surrounds them. Buildings are fixed entities in the minds of most—the notion of mutable space is virtually taboo, even in one's own house. People live in their space with a temerity that is frightening. Home owners generally do little more than maintain their property. It's baffling how rarely the people get involved in fundamentally changing their place by simply undoing it."

"… my preoccupations involve creating deep metamorphic incisions into space/place, I do not want to create a totally new supportive field of vision, of cognition. I want to reuse the old one, the existing framework of thought and sight. So, on the one hand, I am altering the existing units of perception normally employed to discern the wholeness of a thing. On the other hand, much of my life's energies are simply about being denied. There's so much in our society that purposely intends denial: deny entry, deny passage, deny participation, etc. We would all still be living in towers and castles, if we hadn't broken down some of the social and economic barriers, inhibitions, and restraints. My work directly reflects this.

I would like to end with an idea of the direction in which I can see my work evolving. One of the greatest influences on me in terms of new attitudes was a recent experience in Milan. When searching for a factory to 'cut-up,' I found an expansive long-abandoned factory complex that was being exuberantly occupied by a large group of radical Communist youths. They had been taking turns holding down a section of the plant for over a month. Their program was to resist the intervention of 'laissez-faire' real estate developers from exploiting the property. Their proposal was that the area be used for a much needed community services center. My exposure to this confrontation was my first awakening to doing my work, not in artistic isolation, but through an active exchange with people's concern for their own neighborhood. My goal is to extend the Milan experience to the U.S., especially to neglected areas of New York such as the South Bronx where the city is just waiting for the social and physical condition to deteriorate to such a point that the borough can redevelop the whole area into the industrial park they really want. A specific project might be to work with an existing neighborhood youth group and to involve them in converting the all too plentiful abandoned buildings into a social space. In this way, the young could get both practical information about how buildings are made and, more essentially, some first-hand experience with one aspect of the very real possibility of transforming their space. In this way, I could adapt my work to still another level of the given situation. It would no longer be concerned with just personal or metaphoric treatment of the site, but finally responsive to the express will of its occupants."

Work with Abandoned Structures
c. 1975

Work with abandoned structures began with my concern for the life of the city of which a major side effect is the metabolization of old buildings. Here as in many urban centers the availability of empty and neglected structures was a prime textural reminder of the ongoing fallacy of renewal through modernization. The omnipresence of emptiness, of abandoned housing and imminent demolition gave me the freedom to experiment with the multiple alternatives to one's life in a box as well as popular attitudes about the need for enclosure.

Starting small almost to the point of peering through key holes for a better eavesdrop view. I began with a summer of cutting openings into walls and floors that had been staunch defenders of other people's privacy or isolation. By penetrating the layers that divided one family's limited surface reality from another's their simple proximity was heightened. A spacial reality was emphasized that the private pleasures and hells of earlier residents would have never allowed.

The earliest works were also a foray into a city that still was evolving for me. It was an exploration of New York's least remembered parts of the space between the walls of views inside out. I would drive around in my pick-up hunting for emptiness, for a quiet abandoned spot on which to concentrate my piercing attention.

-2-

It was an activity that attempted to transform place into a state of mind by opening walls where doors never were or looking beneath the carpet to clear away the floor.

This initial investigation involved going to the site with saws and taking property apart by removing what in many ways never really belonged to the people who lived there. What a relief to see old joints cracked free! Better to let light pass through a space that still had some of its wits left before its identity would be finally pulverized in the cause of higher efficiency, higher densities. To yield higher mortgage payments, structures built on banking with hot and cold running water. But without getting too sidetracked it is clear that I was helping myself to a last revised point of view of someone else's property—in the final analysis an unpopular way of seeing one's way out of any place in the nick of time.

After an initial group of localized intrusions cut through building surfaces the temptation to encompass a whole place grew. On a trip to Italy in 1973 I was given for the first time a whole house, actually a small office structure standing in the way of a plant expansion, in the highly industrial "Sestri" area of Genoa. The treatment was very simple. A hand-chiseled hole cut through the center of the cement roof and jointed up visually with the interior walls by an intersection of horizontal and vertical incisions.

-3-

The project was composed of these two treatments "Atrium Roof" and "Datum Cut" which went a long way towards defunctualizing this engineering building. The structure was cored; walls and doors, roof and ceiling were united by a centralized opening; it was no longer a building to separate owners from workers but a hub around which nothing but light worked. The issue of locating and redefining the center of a whole structure has carried over into two more recent works. "Splitting" and "Bingo" both done about a year ago. Here for the first time the area was black ghetto suburbia or small-town America. So the identity of these buildings corresponded to a unit situation that dominates the countryside in the U.S. Here no longer enclosure per se but containerization and the ubiquitous object house became the subject matter. No manipulation made so far can be stronger than the object's identity, including a violent bulldozing. For even when flattened and cleared the scar still reads house. In both projects nothing more than a modest shift of structure and perception could be hoped for amidst the all-pervasive suburban texture. Working with the common house for all it enlists of heart and mind was for me as much a kind of juggling act in which as familiar objects swirl even to a blur they remain unchanged.

But the quixotic activity of dancing around those structures was the basic non-abstraction of the two projects.

-4-

Confronting the house by activating the space around it so that internal changes also became strong external images. A process that while it goes on in design has critically different implications in these works.

The activities involved in unbuilding these two projects were cutting and moving the building parts around a center. The first of these works was "Splitting" done in Englewood, New Jersey; it involved cutting the building in half from its gaggle to its latch and from room to basement using two vertical parallel cuts one inch apart. Then by beveling down the foundations the rear half was tilted back, causing the double line to open into a split. So while this small not so happy house got cut and shifted out of place, the action took only minutes of the building's history. Yet by my view all those pent-up lives respecting the tiny cramped rooms were suddenly flooded with direct sunlight.

The last of these "house" projects "Bingo" was done in Niagara Falls, New York. In America "Bingo" is a weekly church function—serious kicks for the Christian aged. Only the hotels that used to house honeymooners are being cleared away for a more serious renewed urban center. The "Bingo" that I planned on 419 Erie Ave. encompassed ten days of maneuvering over the north facade measuring out a nine part grid of equal 5' × 9' rectangles.

-5-

These fragments were removed one at a time in rotation around the center leaving it undisturbed in position until the building was demolished. The life of this project once finished was twelve hours. Even before the last section to be removed had been crated, the bulldozer crew arrived tearing up buildings and trees to either side of the project. By six p.m. their machinery was still but only until six the next morning, during which time my crew worked to finish documentation or move crates with barely any time to view the final result. All crated sections 1/9 through 8/9 were then moved to a site along the Niagara river where they were dumped to function as a "double—sculpture garden" until the combined growth and disintegration reclaims the ensemble.

(I hope you can glean from this rough ramble enough information to help describe some of the nature of these works. I am sure corrections, improvement and clarifications will have to be made for I have no illusions about my struggles with writing around the work.)

Berlin Wall: If We Follow the Wall
1976

If we follow the wall from its origins as a patchwork rush job an emergency effort to fill up the gaps to stem the tide, then it is a magnificent wall as it has grown taller and slimmer and whiter in spiritual harmony with a physically as well as morally reconstructed city. There is no work that matches its shameless grace which now runs in smooth serpentine curves through the city. It has reached maturity and runs an elaborate course with new authority in a tasteful mixture of bank vaults, prison walls and pure art. As the old clumsy cinderblocks are replaced with new precast slabs the Berliners dull or oblivious sense of its presence is heightened, rekindled into a captive round of applause especially for the children who play along it and the patient vigilant army who caress it with their aimed binoculars from within or without. Of course some have chosen the luxury of hiding it behind bushes or trees while …

Elegance. I wondered who it is for, who is the architect of this labor of blinded love. Such a creative monument cannot be without its personalities, without its inspired originators but in a magnanimous act of community spirit the pleasure of its inventors remains anonymous. It is true the older wall had a folksy rustic finish that if decorated with vines or just left to weather can be followed like the absolutely normal walls to any baronial estate but because of hasty technique the result falls within the international junk-yard style. Until one sees the other side. As an equal opportunity employer it is marvelous how well the labor force is served by such a man power consumer.

I would suggest that as things are looking up at the wall that a bi-annual effort is made to increase its height and purpose by incorporating more useful spaces into its mass. You have to hand it to them where New York can't even pave a road from one year to the next, the brains behind the wall have managed to clear a swath at least 100 yards wide through seventy miles of well populated streets.

If we follow this wall from its origins as an emergency patchworked, rush job, a drastic effort to fill up the gaps, to stem the tide, then its magnificence stands proud in its shopping market ferro-concrete newness—especially as it has grown taller and slimmer and whiter in spiritual harmony with a show place city. It is the moral and physical renewal of a pre-world war Bauhaus vision. The German design machine has conquered America and the world only to return to Berlin is through its wall. There are few works other than walls that command such shameless grace especially the new one that divides this queen of Europe as it unfolds its smooth serpentine curves of authority. Its appeal evolves from the imitative successes of the eastern Berlin Democratic Republic in projecting a tasteful mixture of bank vaulting, penitentiary walls and pure art upon its western frontier.

PLATES

Gordon Matta-Clark, *Facade Theater Drop*, 1974

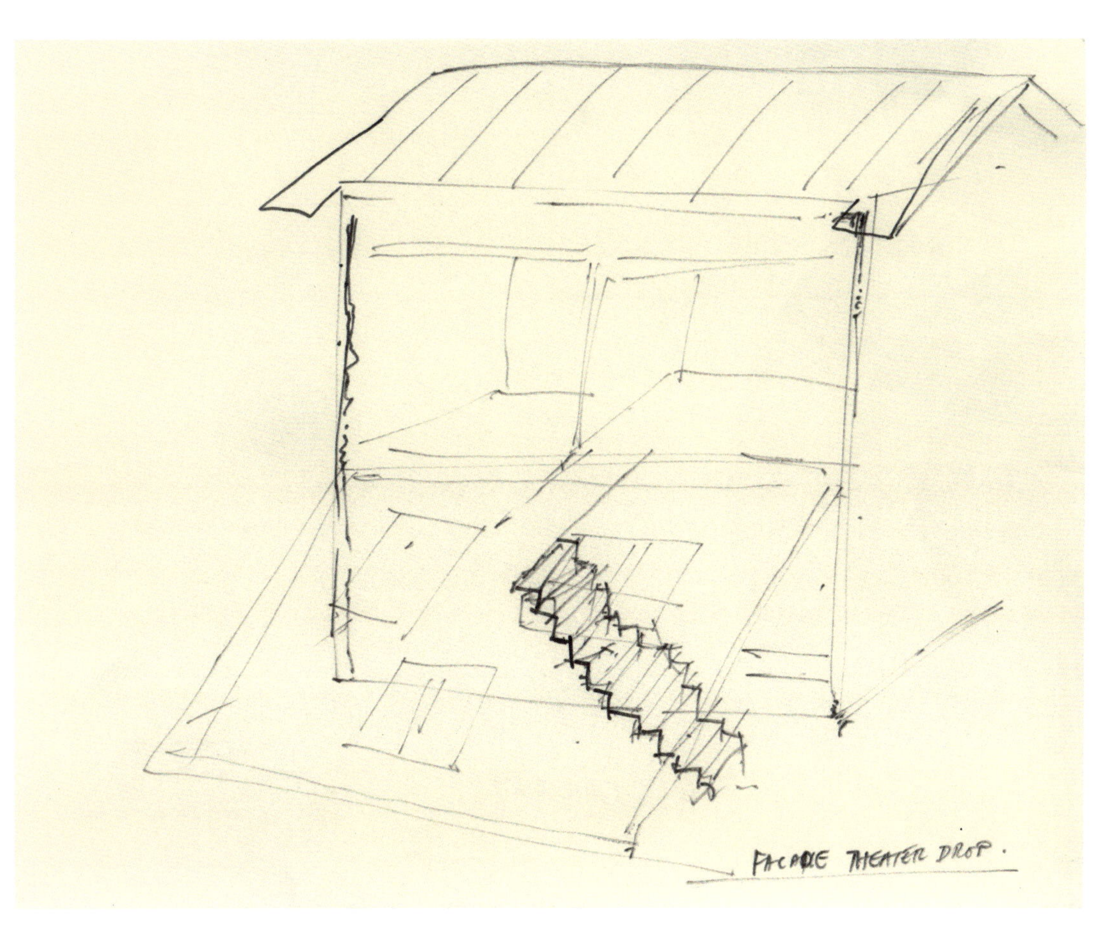

FACADE THEATER DROP.

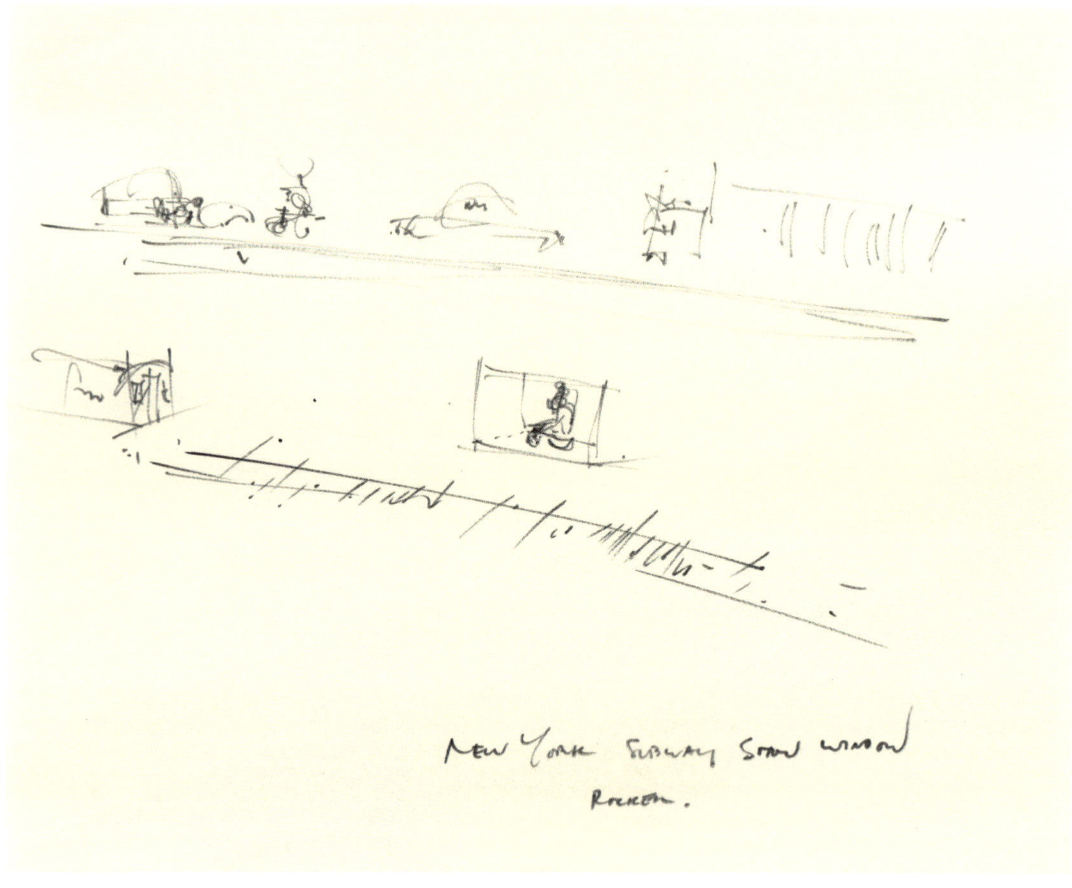

Gordon Matta-Clark, *New York Subway Show Window Rocker*, 1974

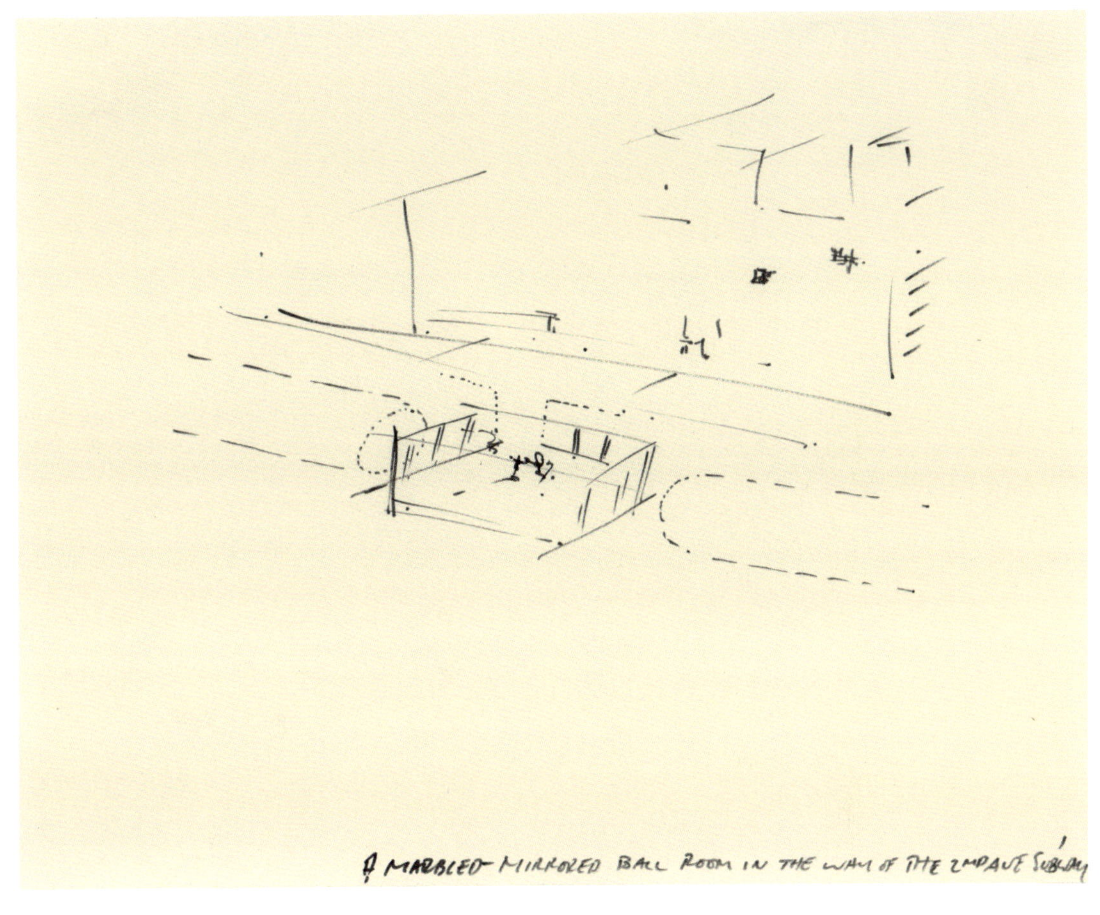

Gordon Matta-Clark, *A Marbled Mirrored Ball Room in the Way of the 2nd Avenue Subway*, 1974

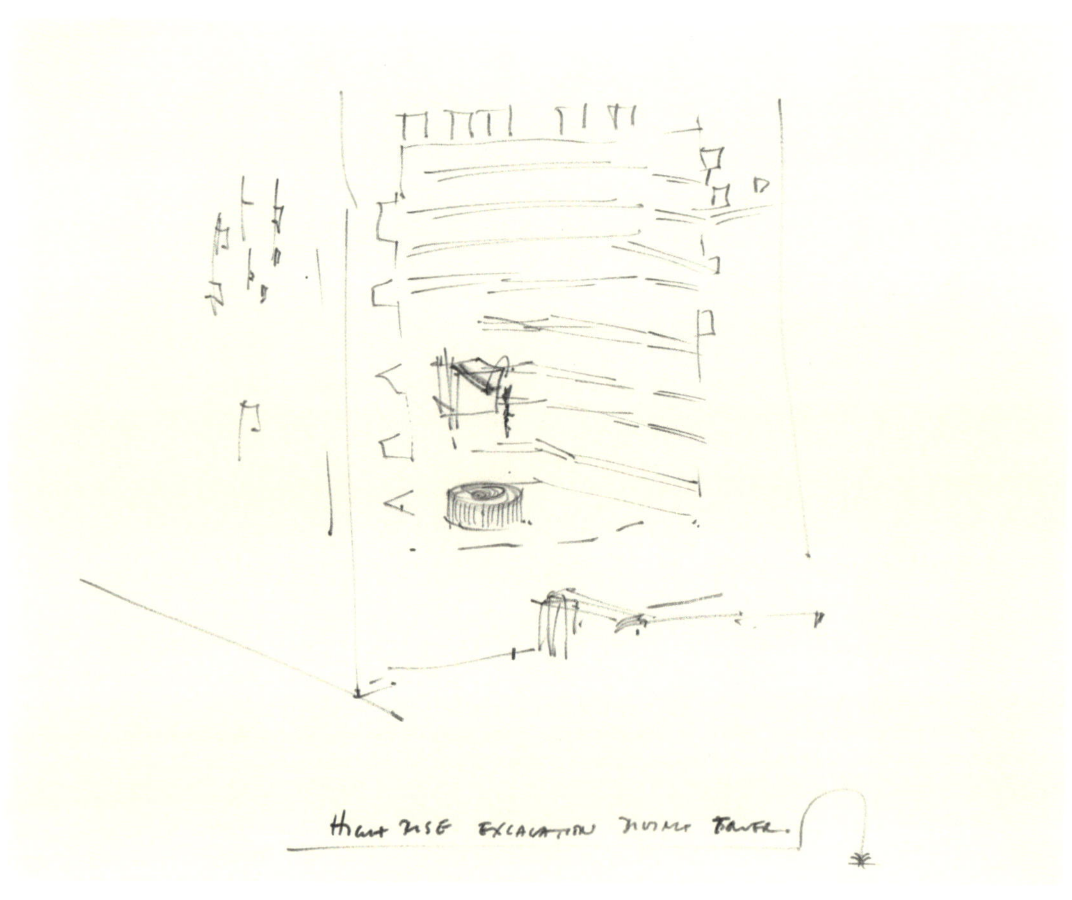

Gordon Matta-Clark, *High-Rise Excavation Diving Tower*, 1974

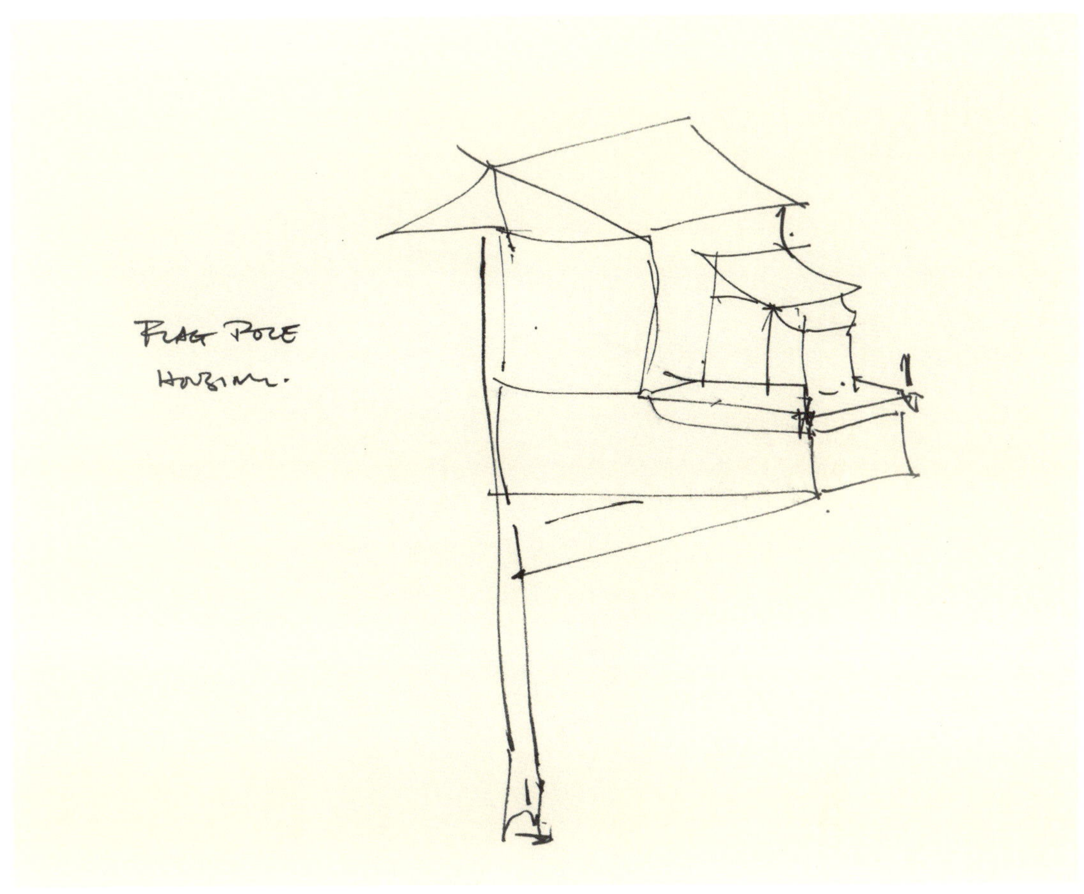

Gordon Matta-Clark, *Flag Pole Housing*, 1974

Gordon Matta-Clark, *Fresh Air Cart*, 1974

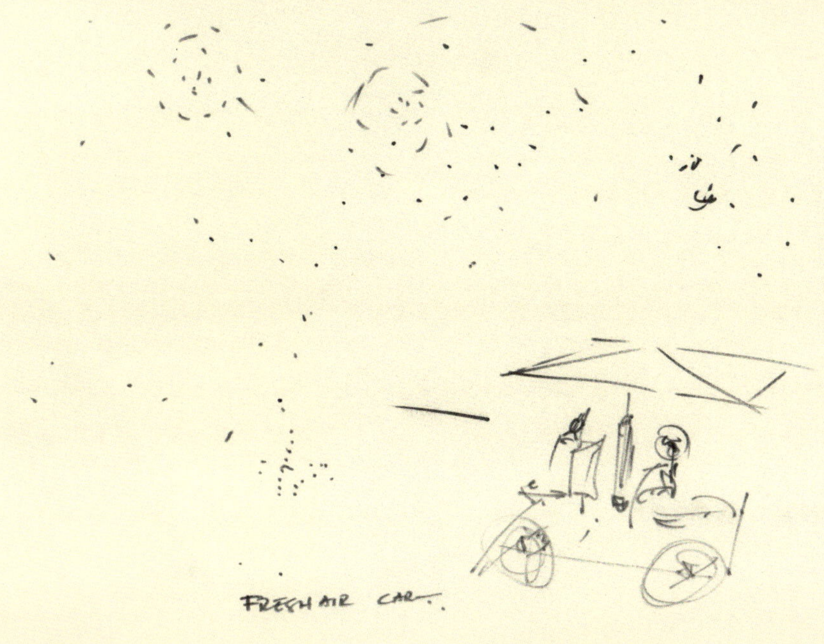
FRESH AIR CART.

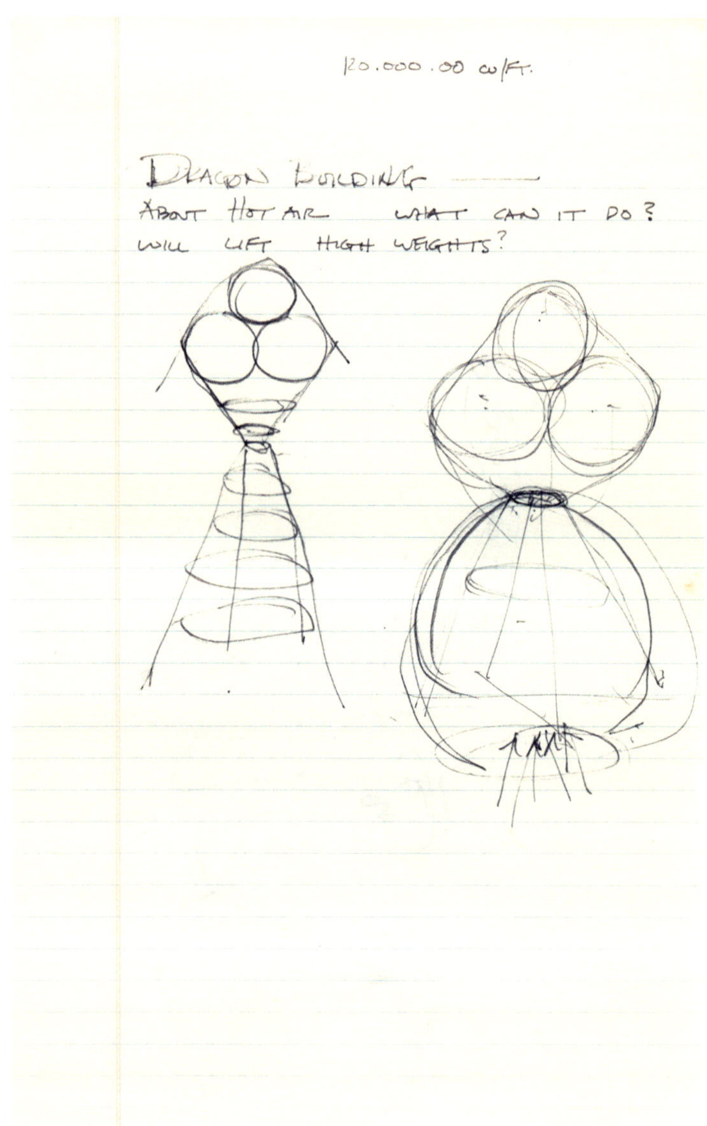

Gordon Matta-Clark, *Dragon Building*, 1978

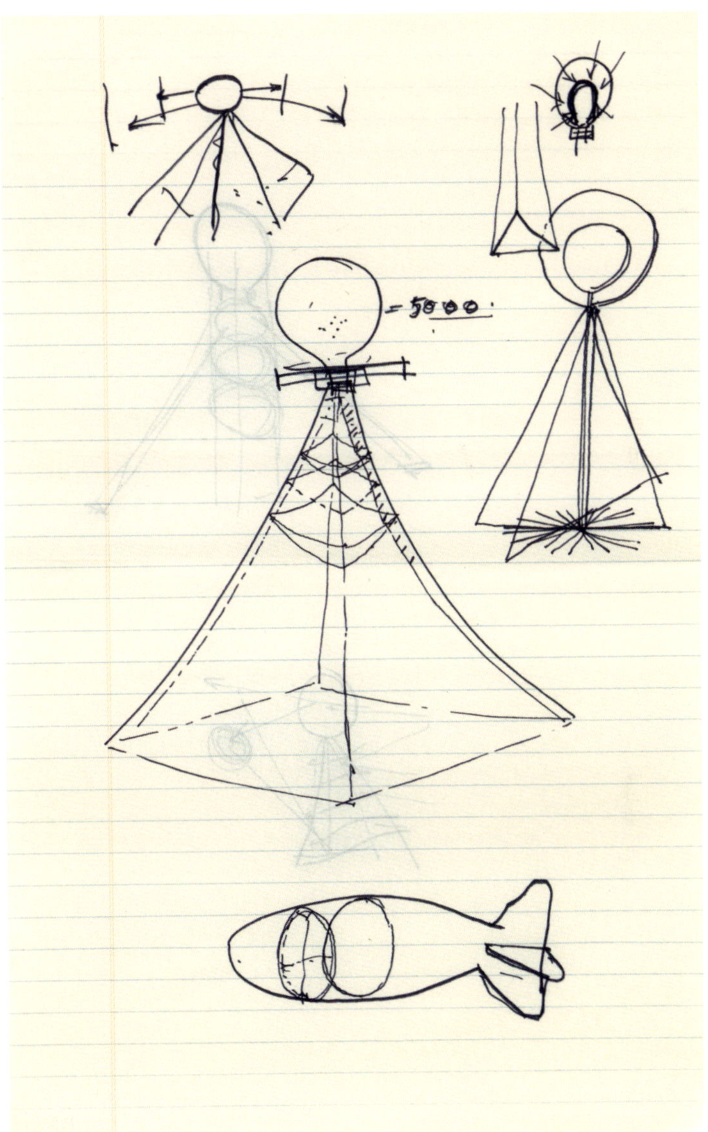

Gordon Matta-Clark, *Dragon Building*, 1978

Gordon Matta-Clark, *Dragon Building*, 1978

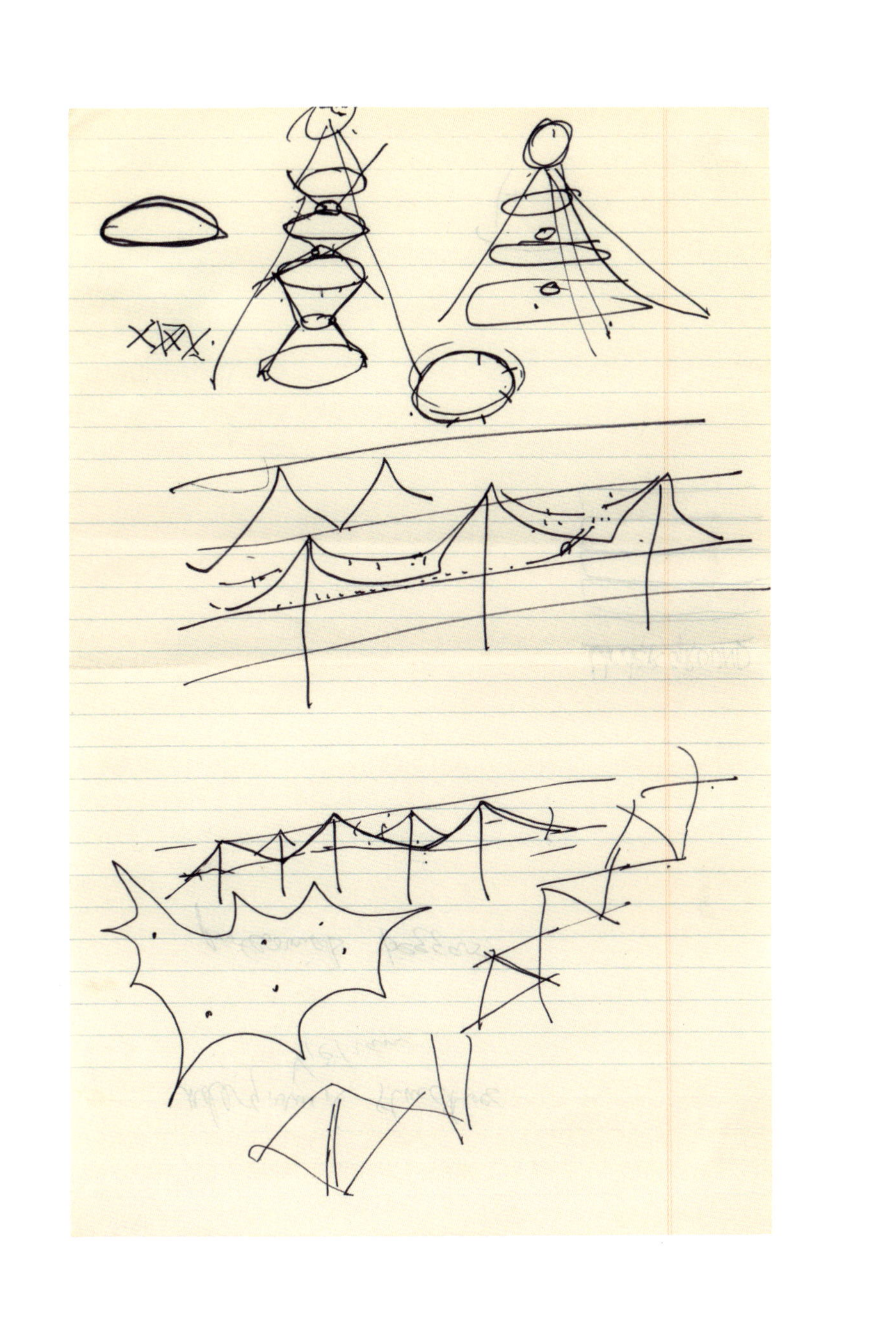

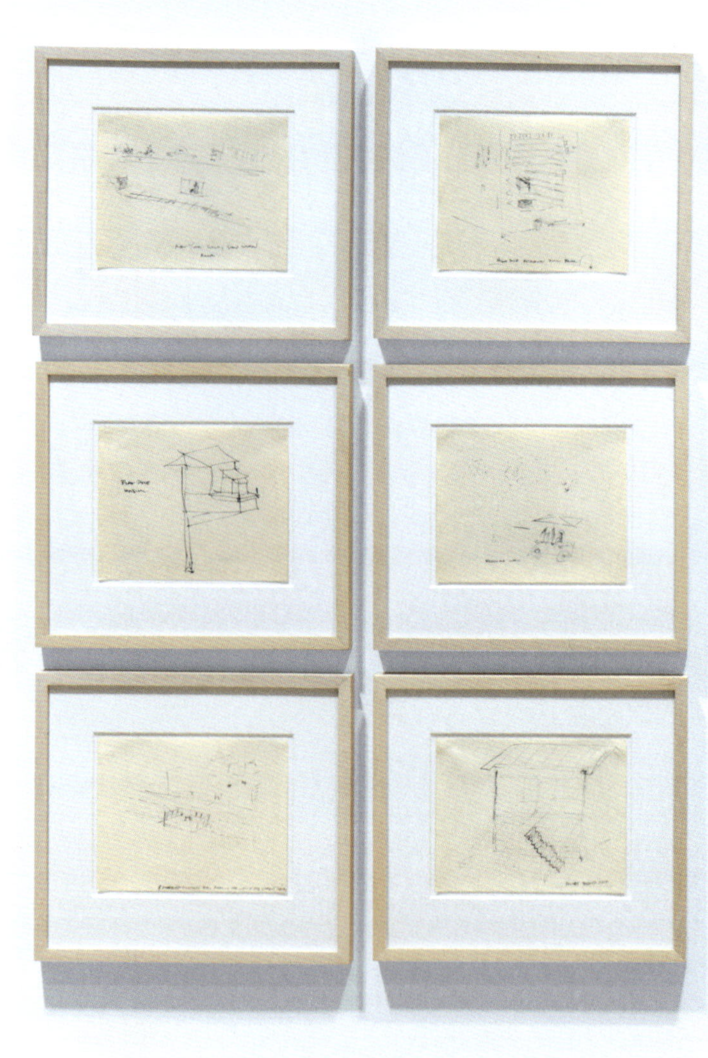

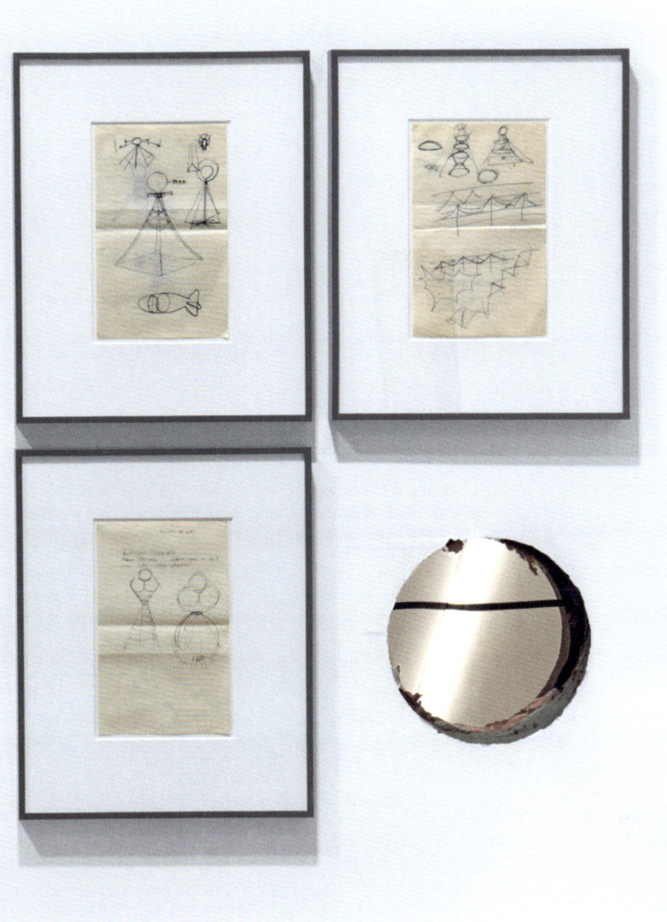

Gordon Matta-Clark, *Untitled (Cut Drawing)*, 1973

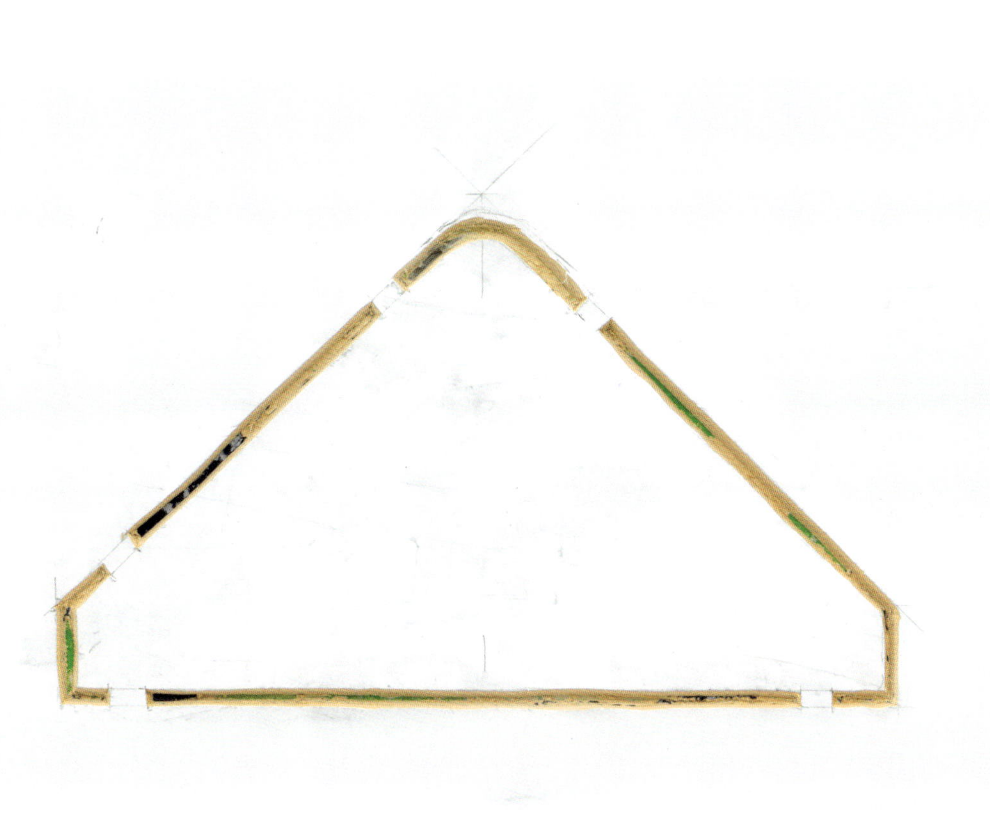

Gordon Matta-Clark, *A W-Hole House (Four Corners)*, 1973

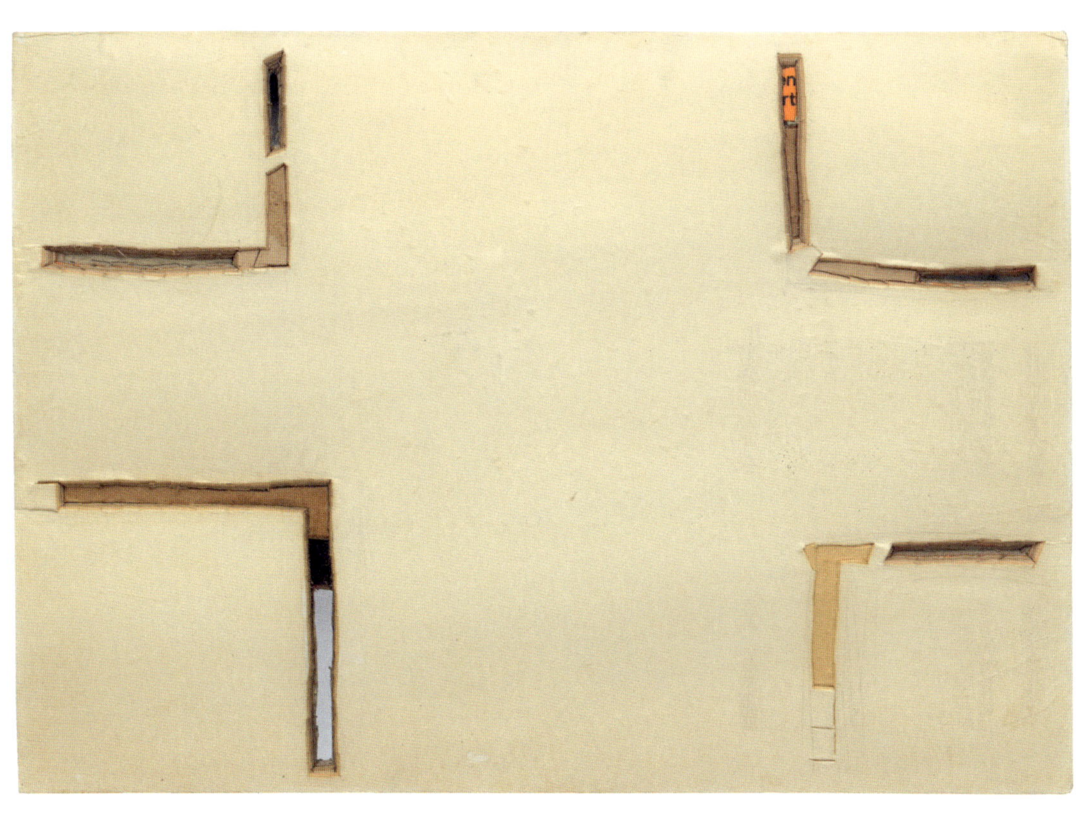

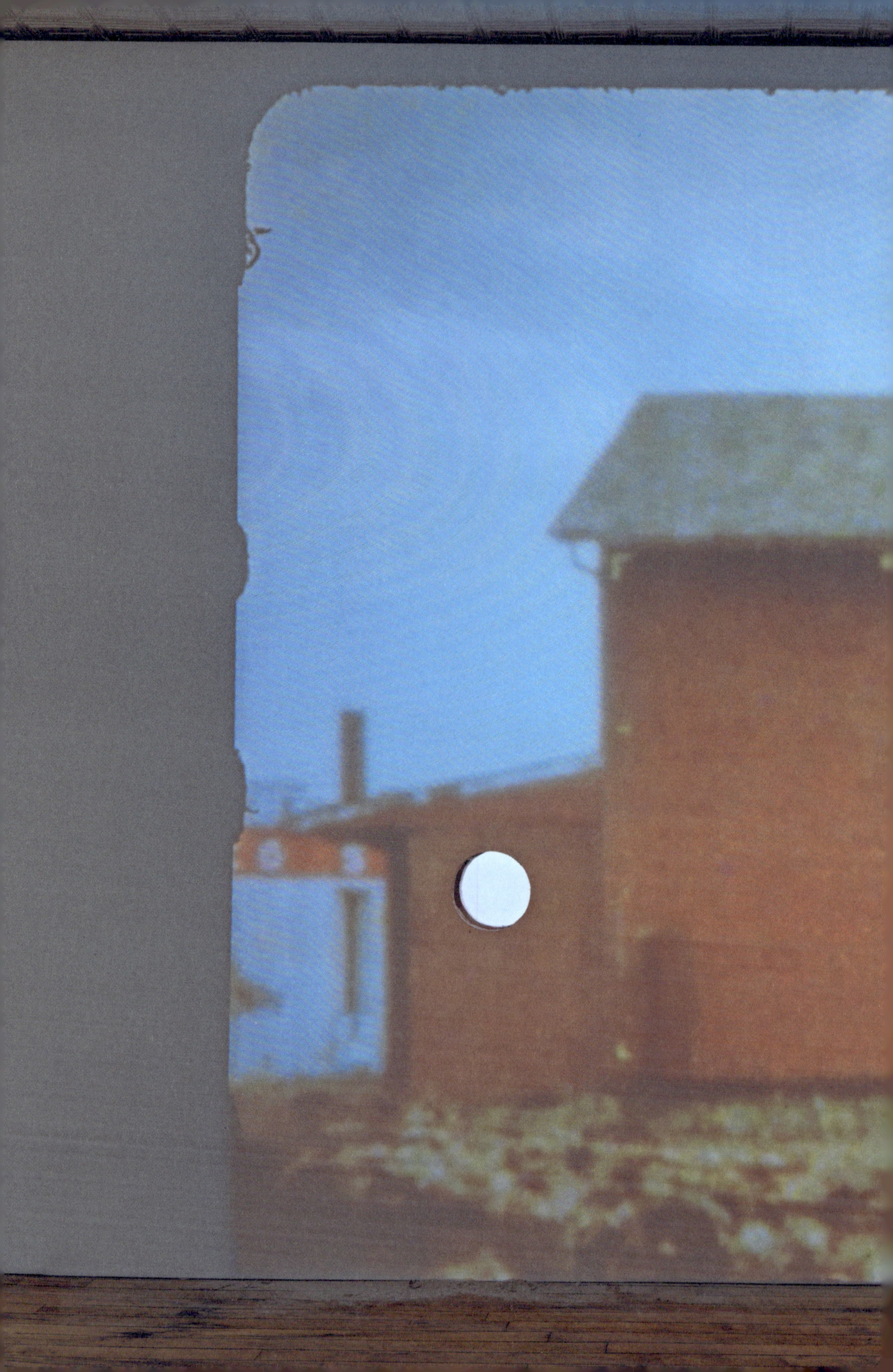

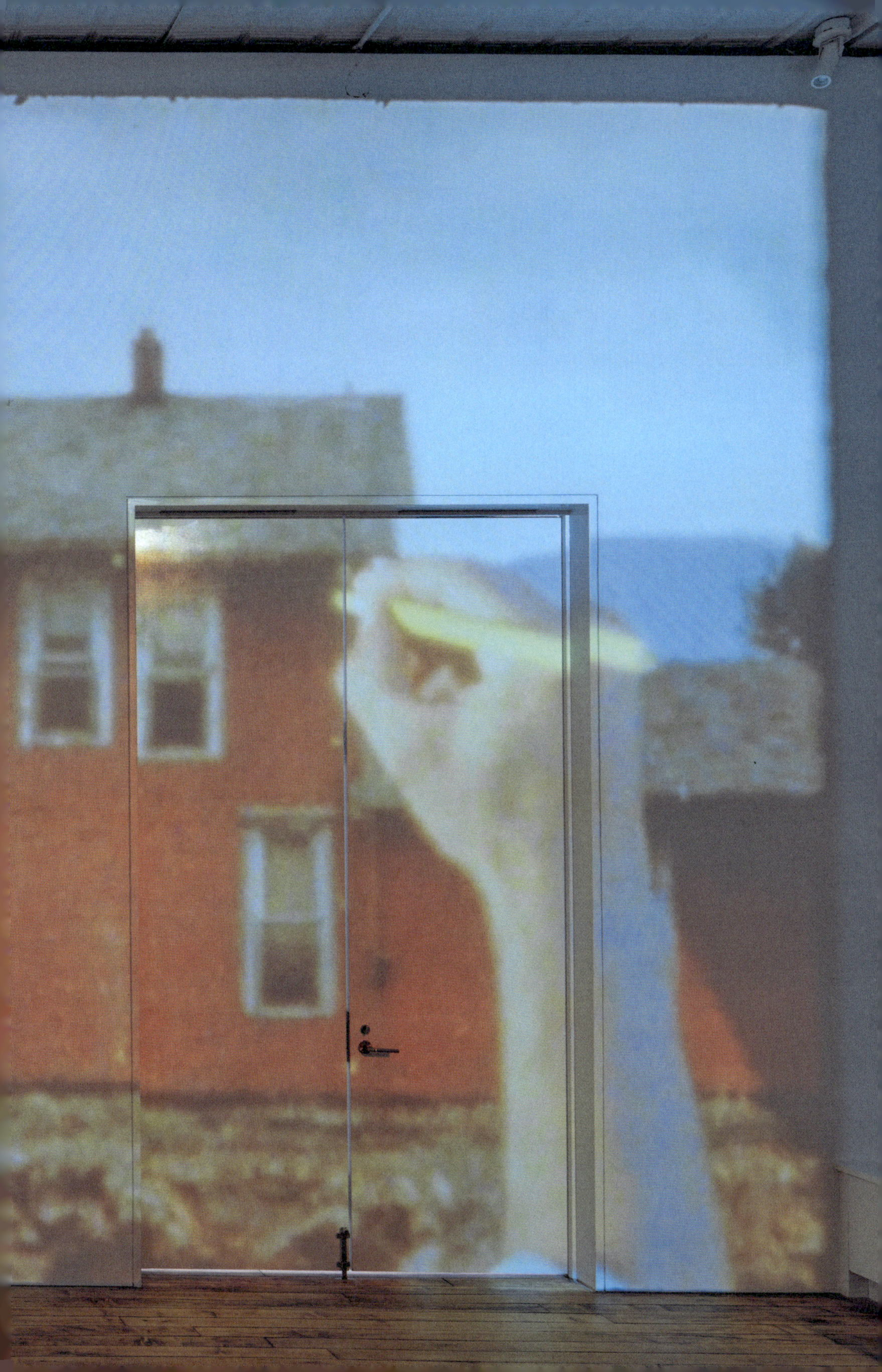

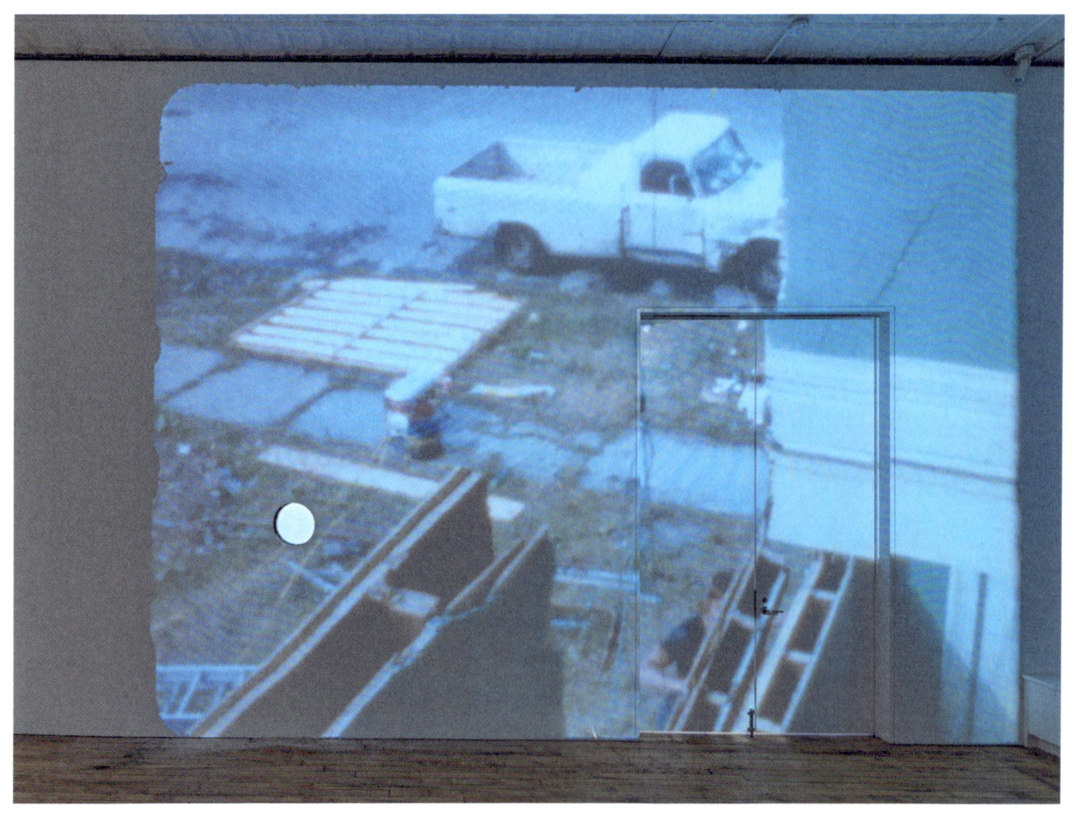

Pages 48–51
Gordon Matta-Clark, *Bingo X Ninths*, 1974

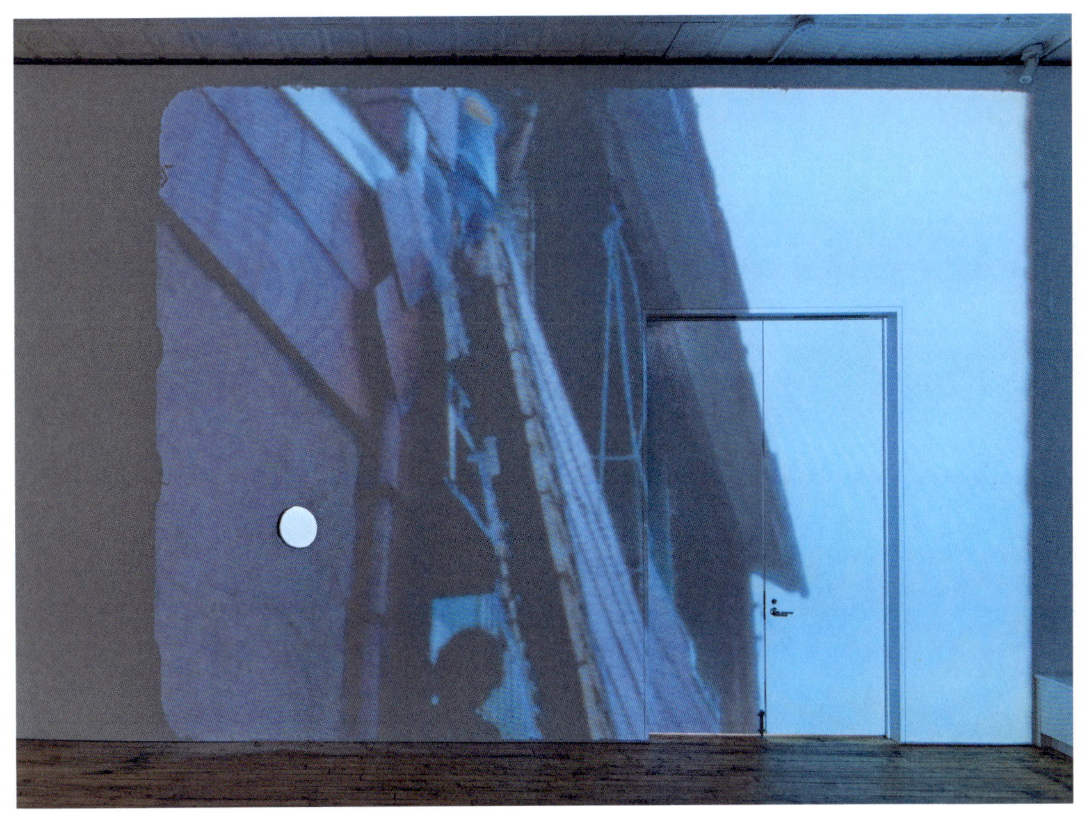

Pages 52–53
Gordon Matta-Clark, *Conical Intersect*, 1975

Pages 54–61
Pope.L, *Vigilance a.k.a. Dust Room*, 2023

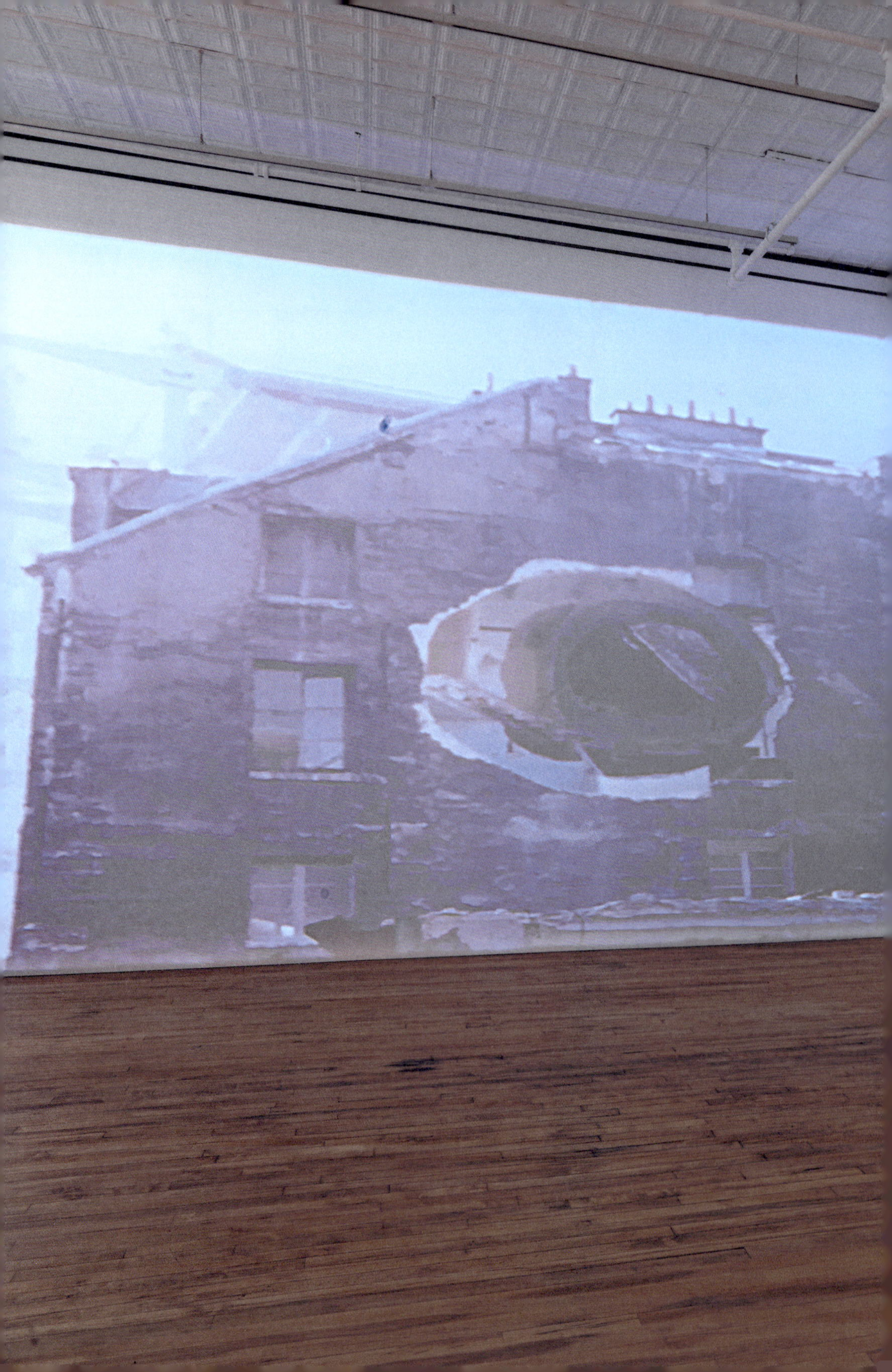

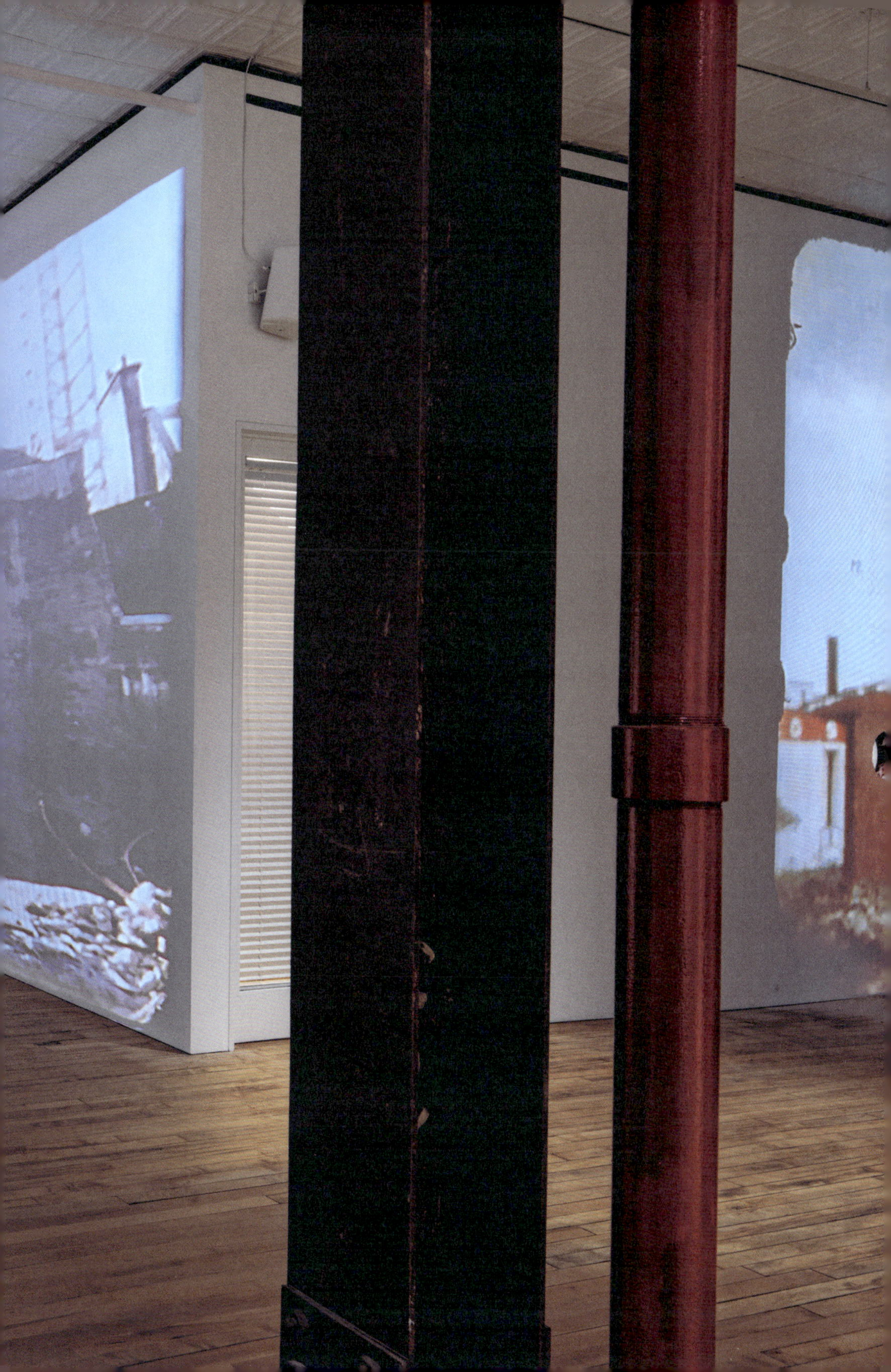

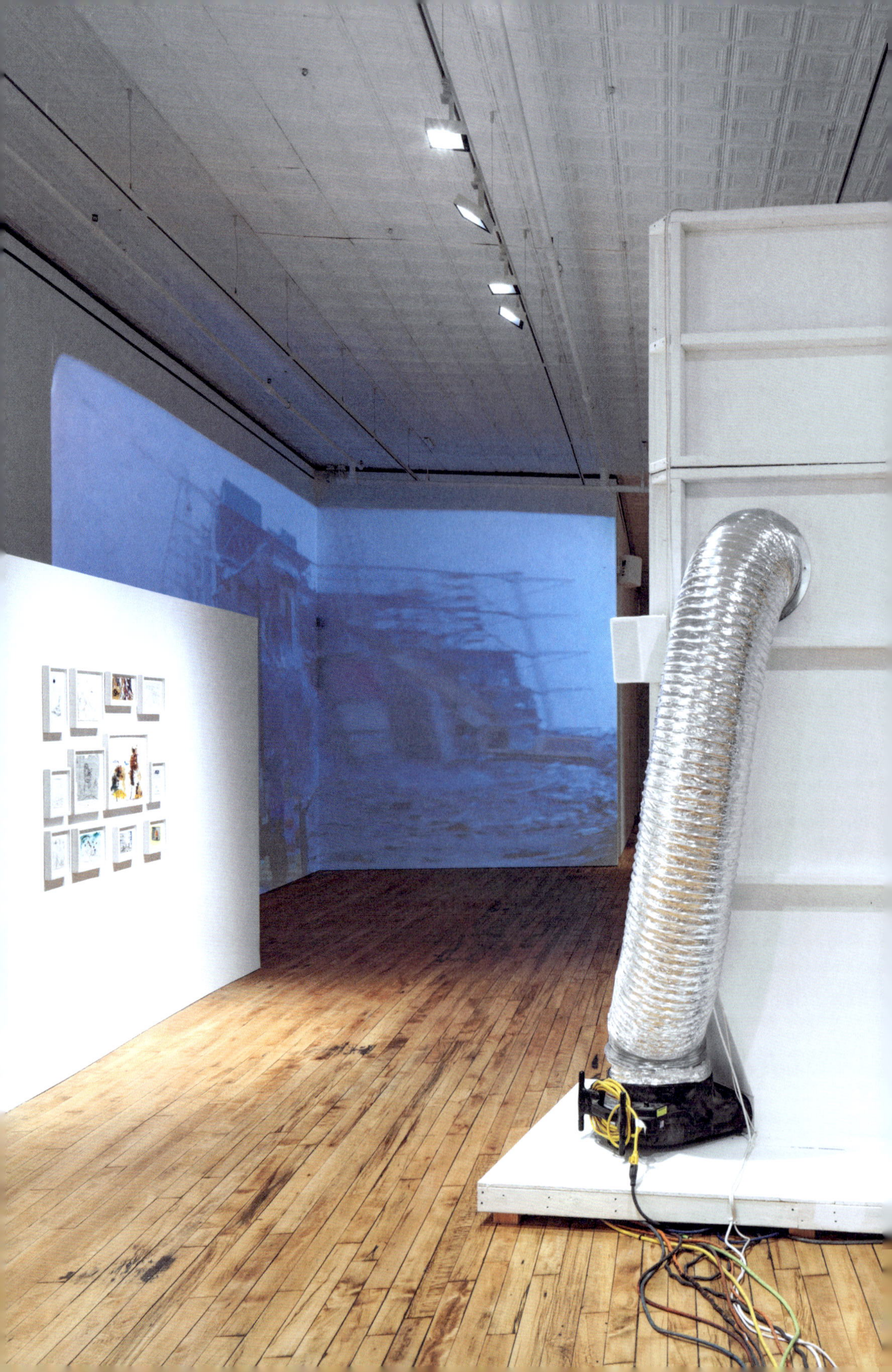

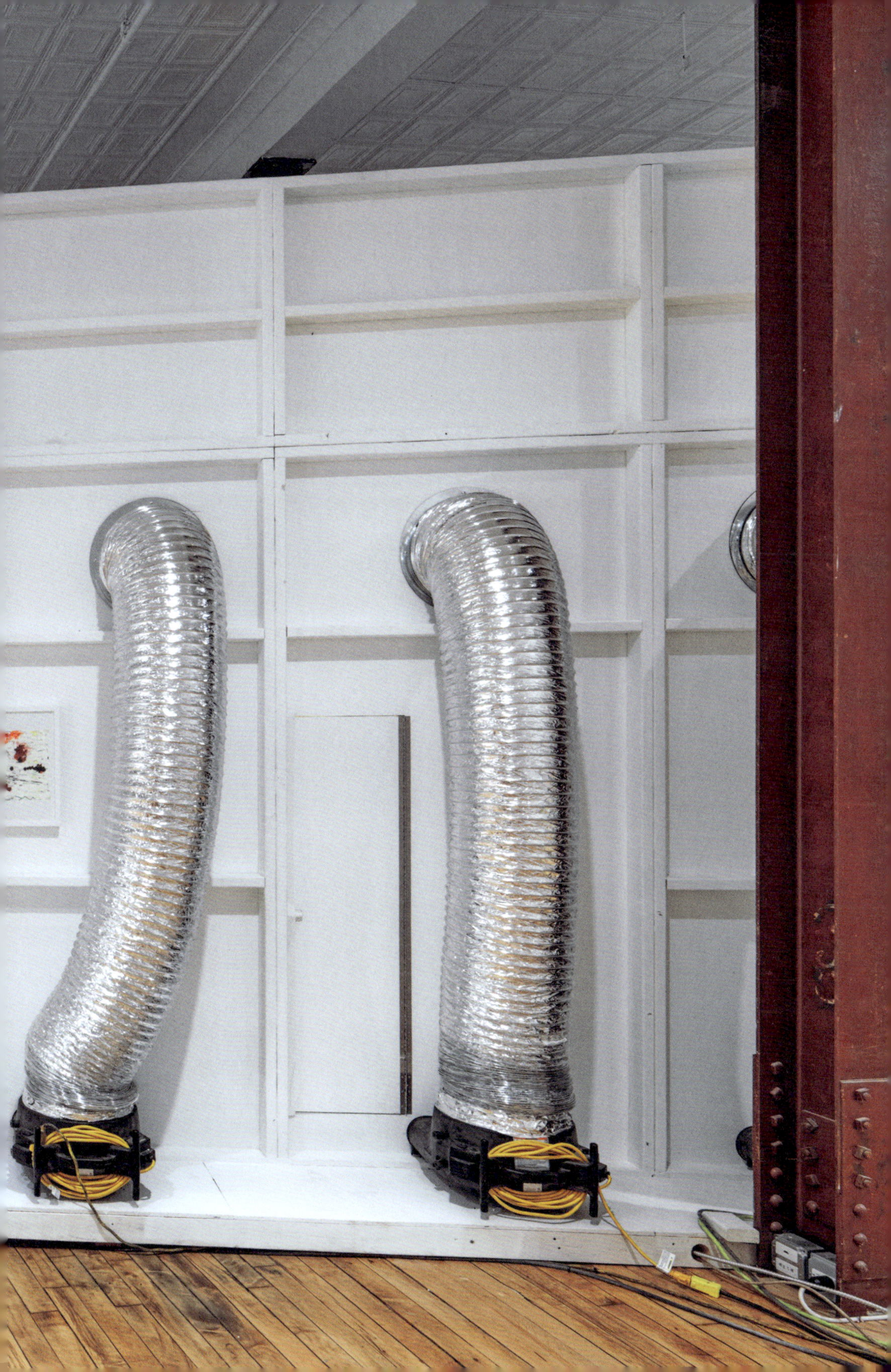

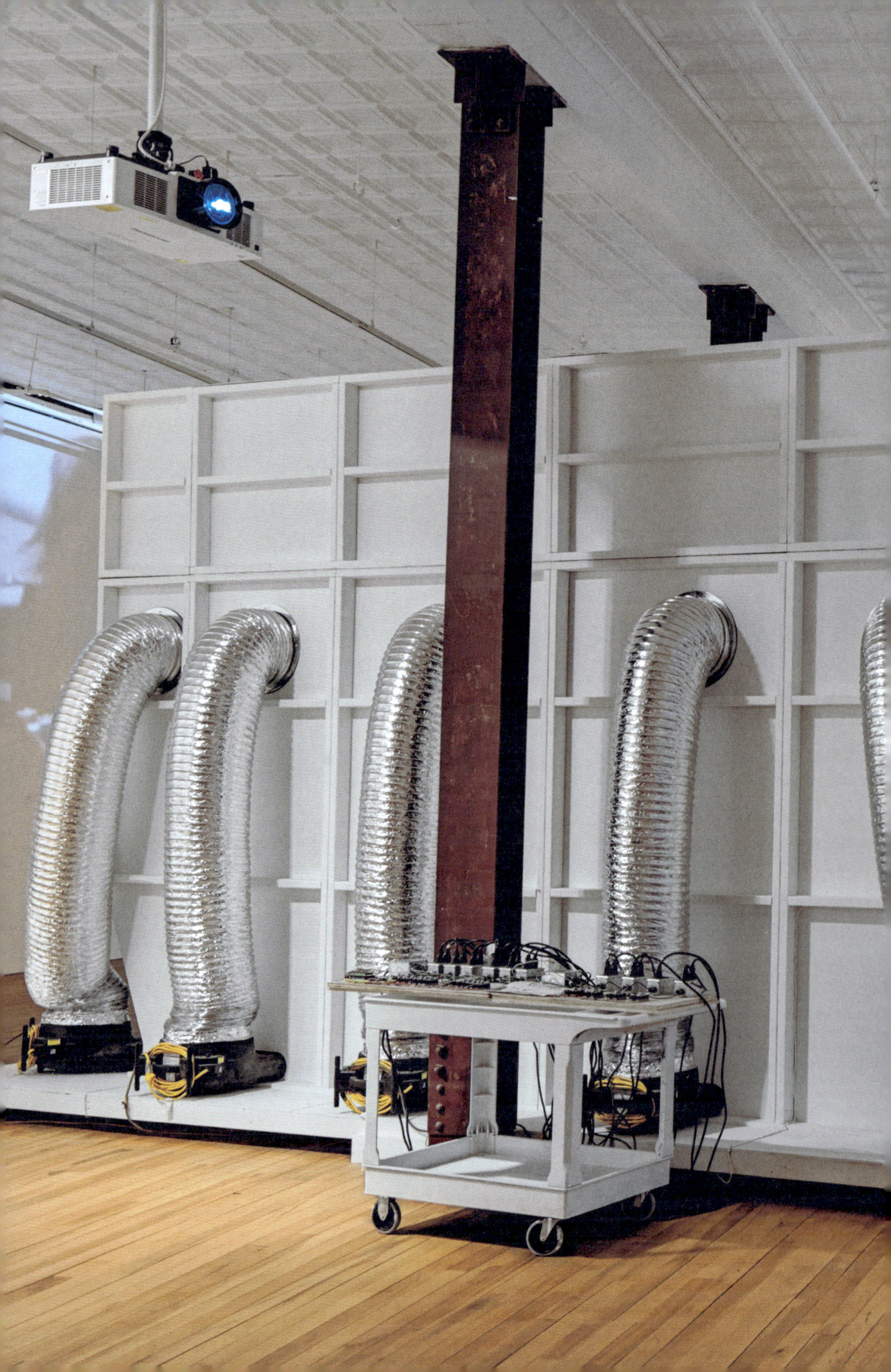

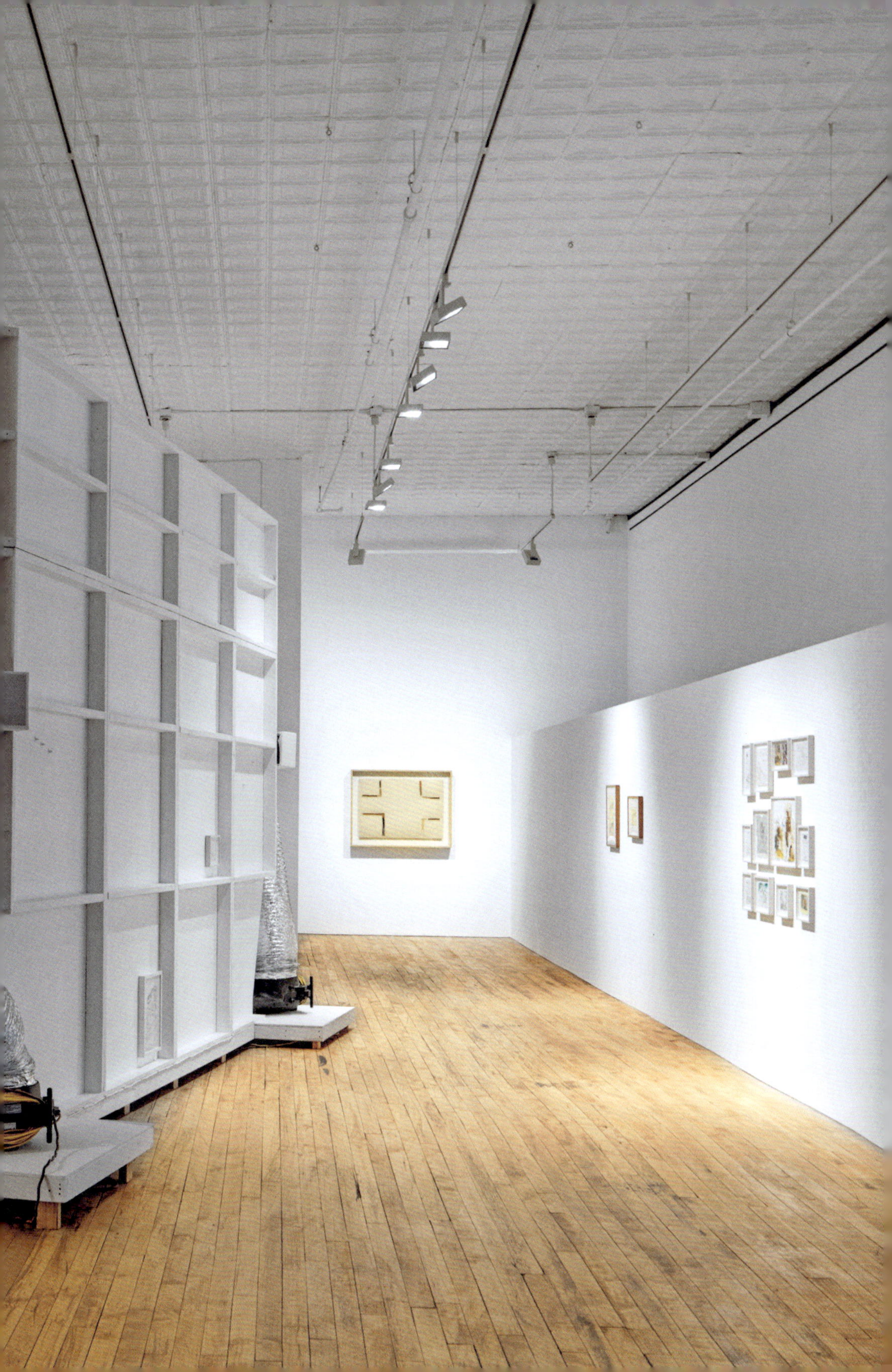

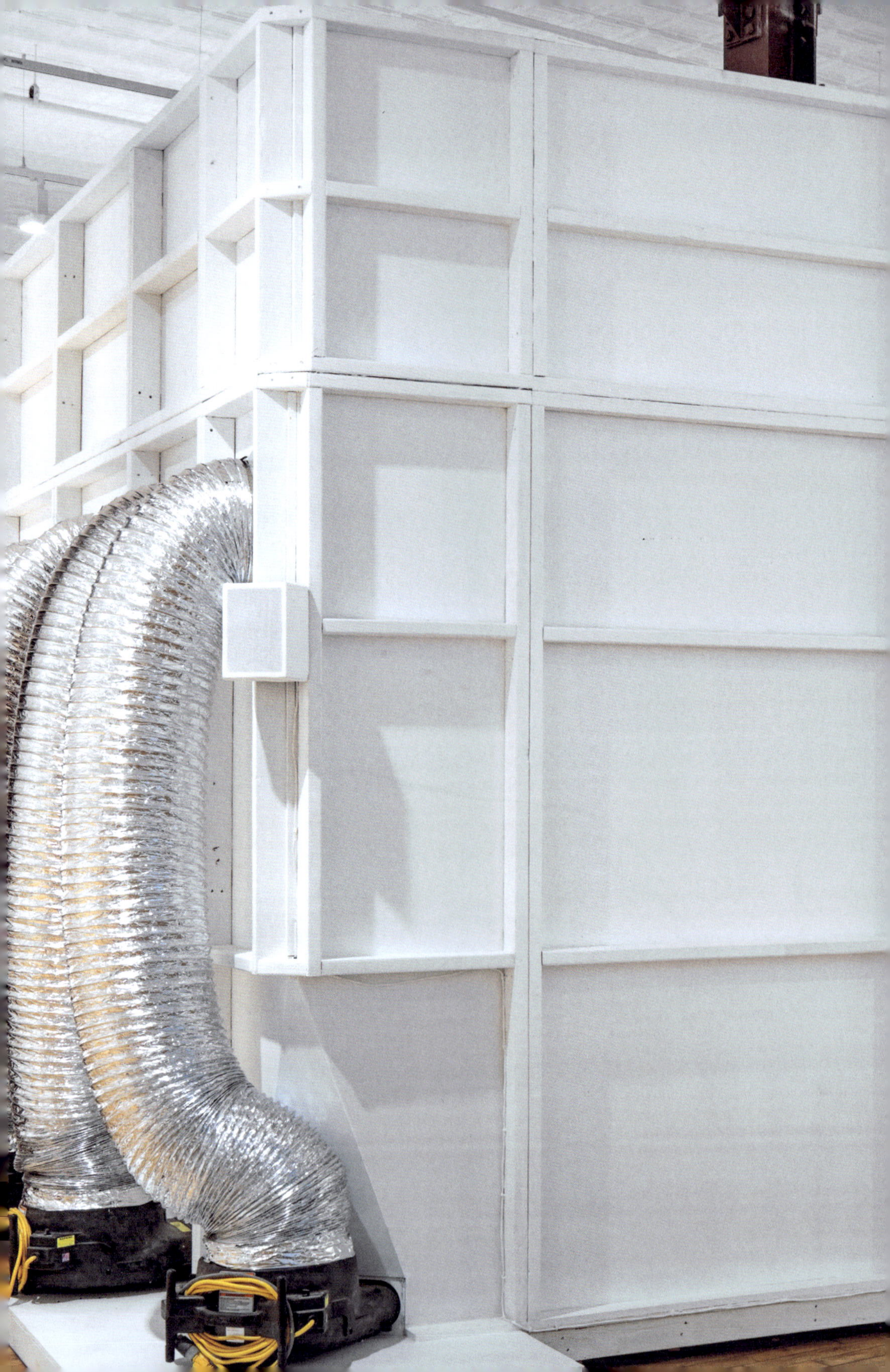

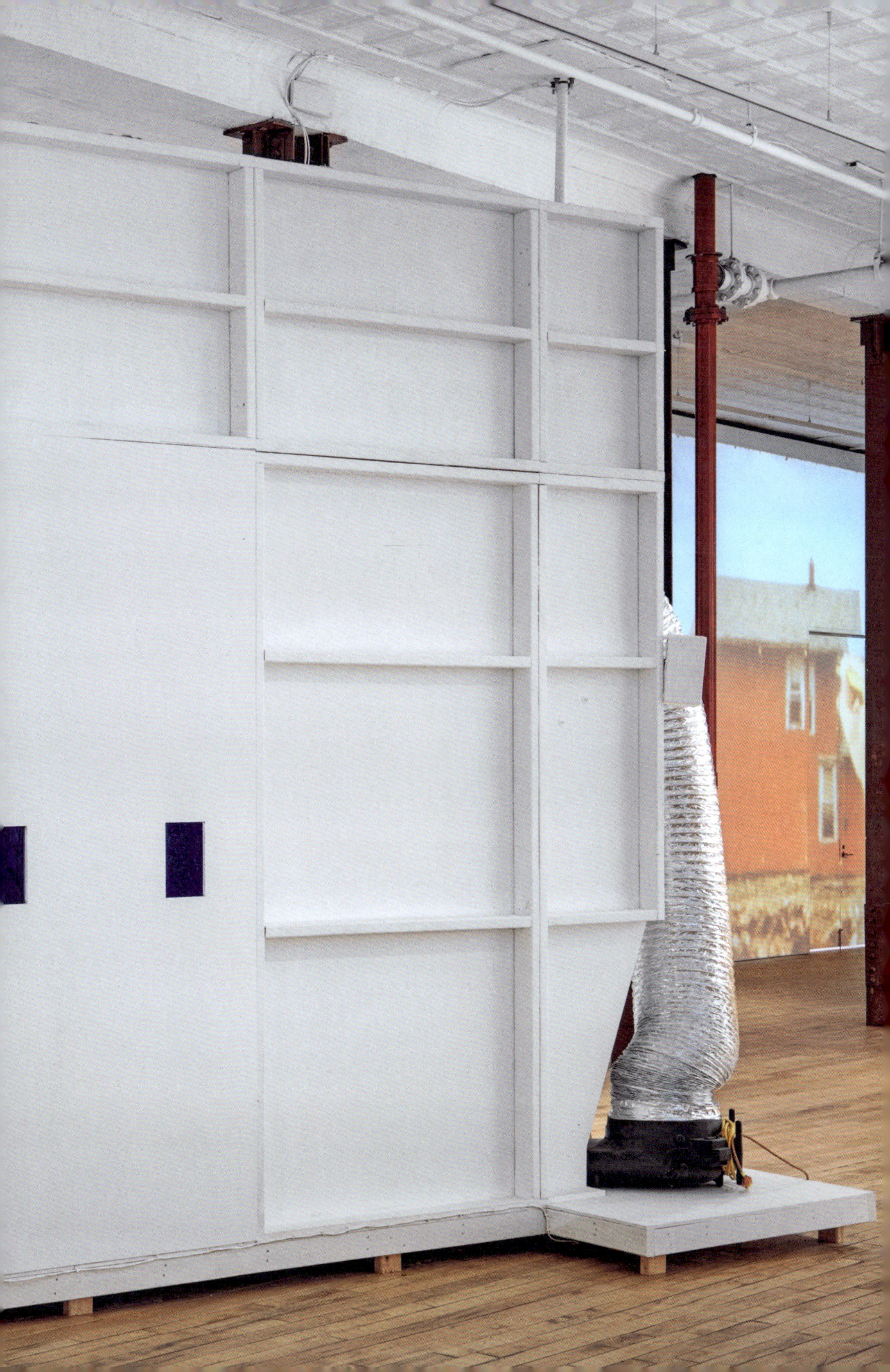

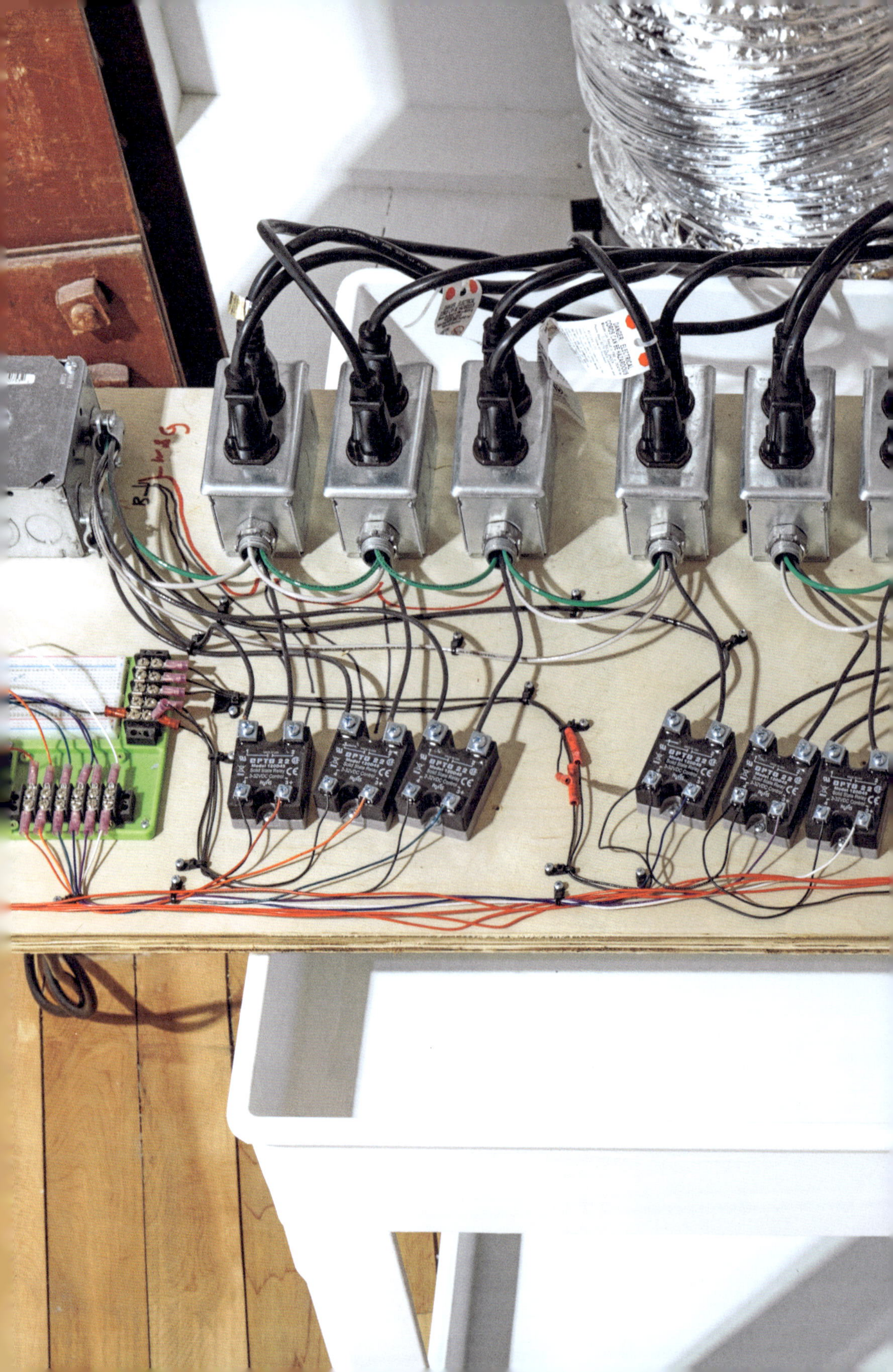

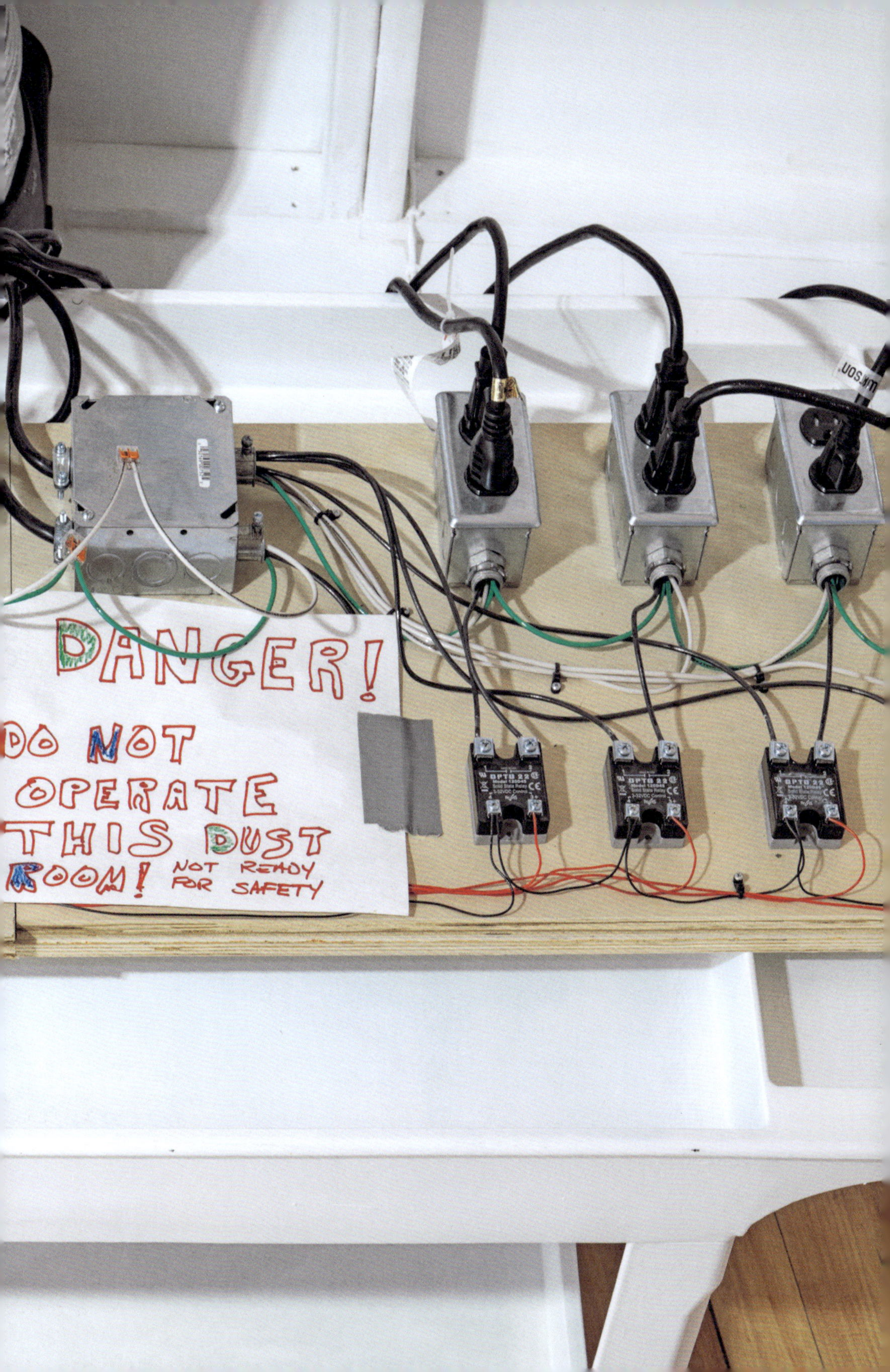
DANGER!
DO NOT
OPERATE
THIS DUST
ROOM! NOT READY
FOR SAFETY

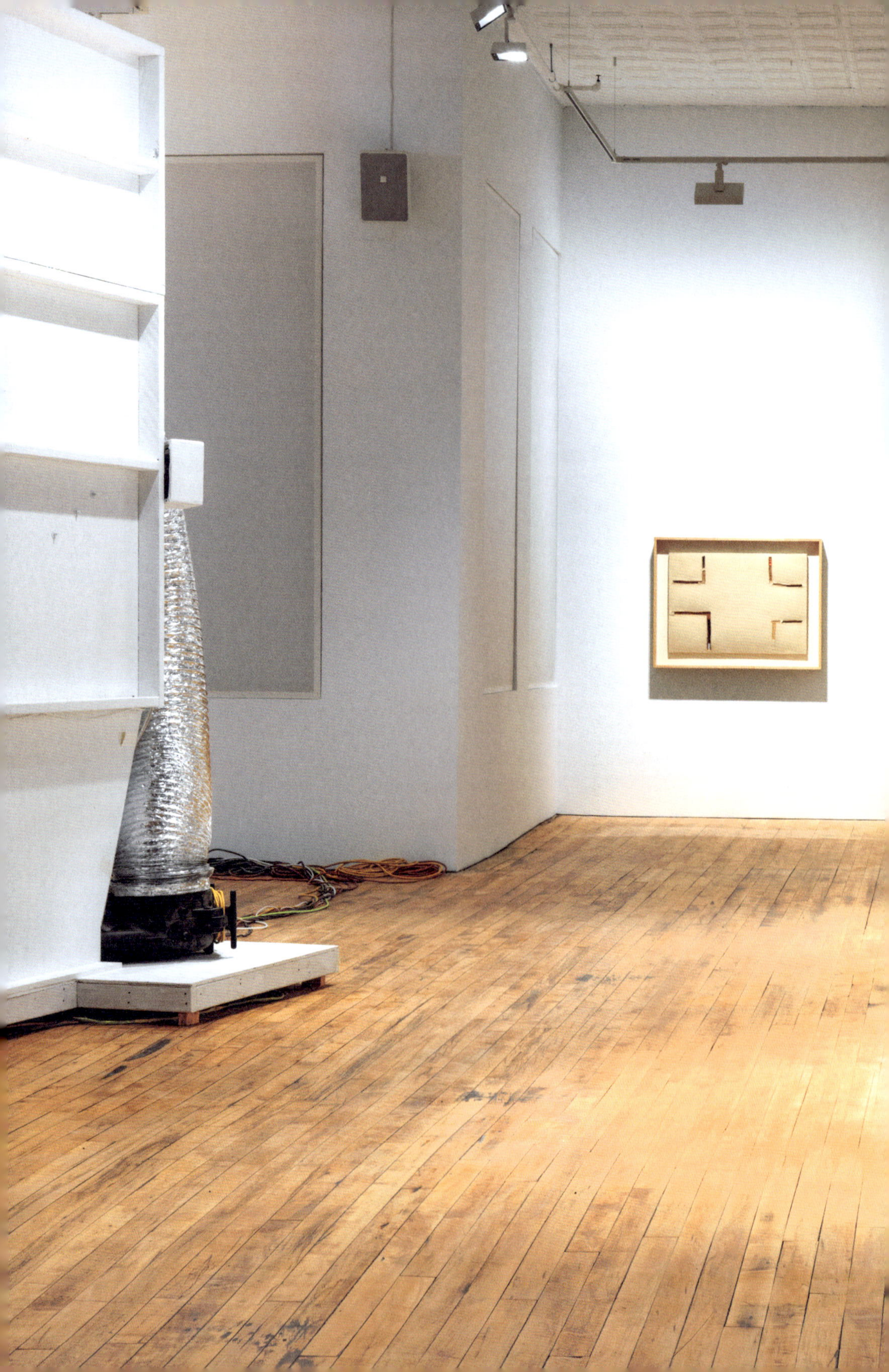

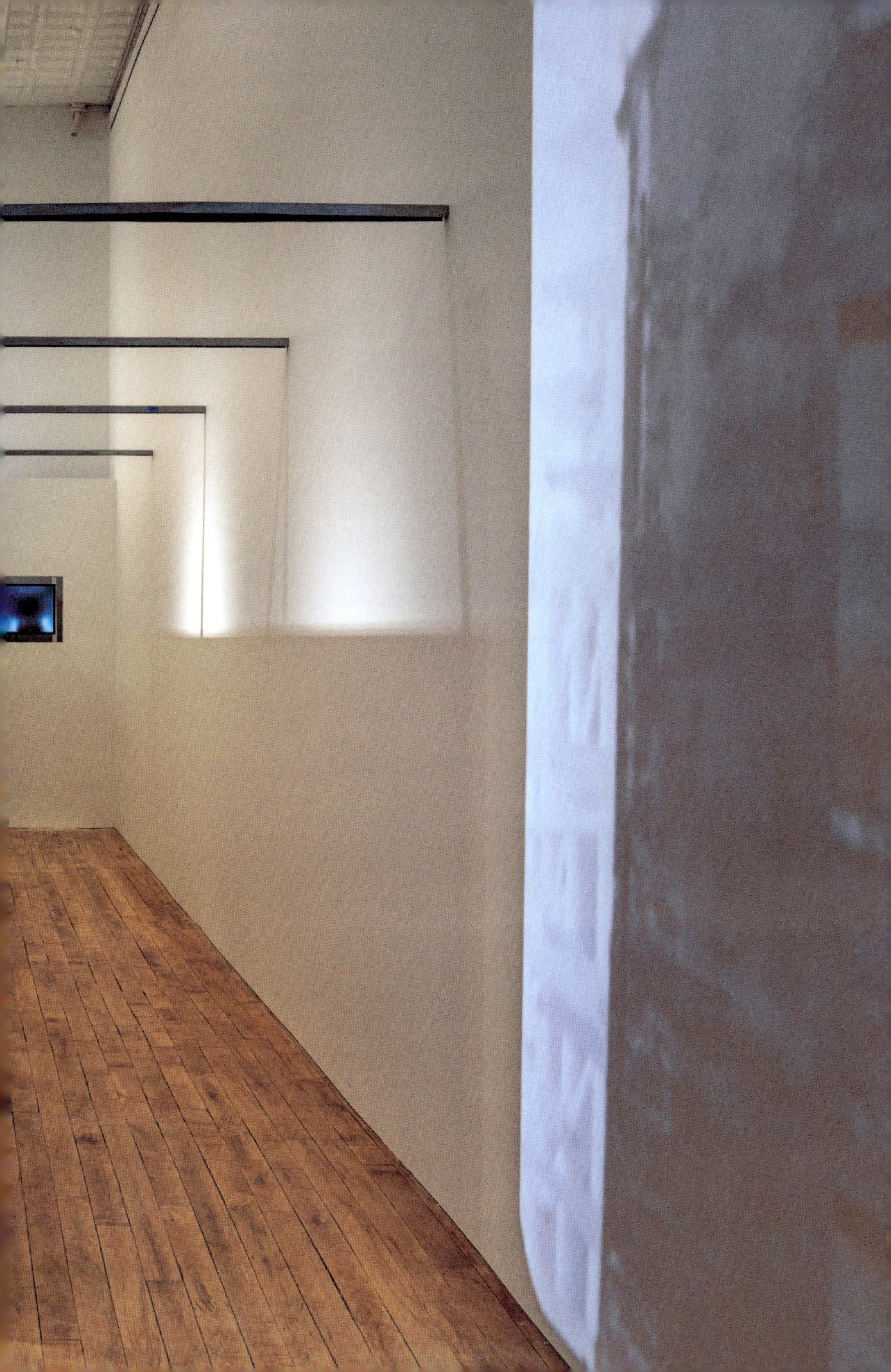

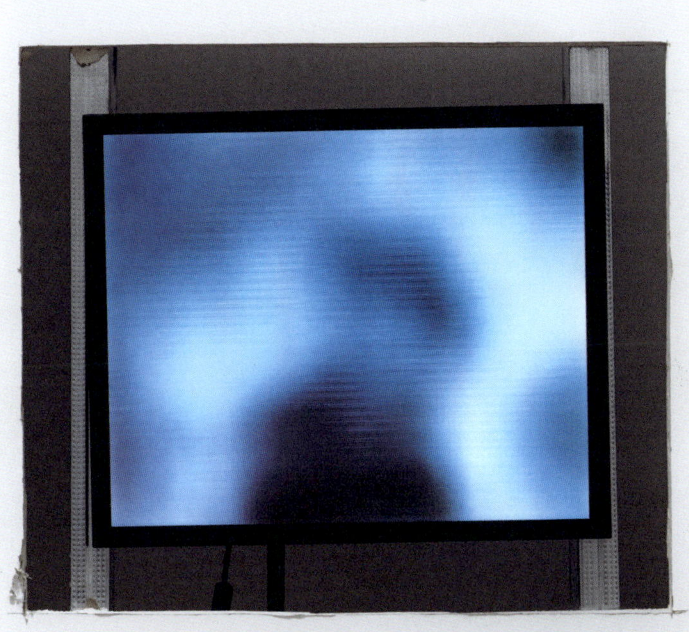

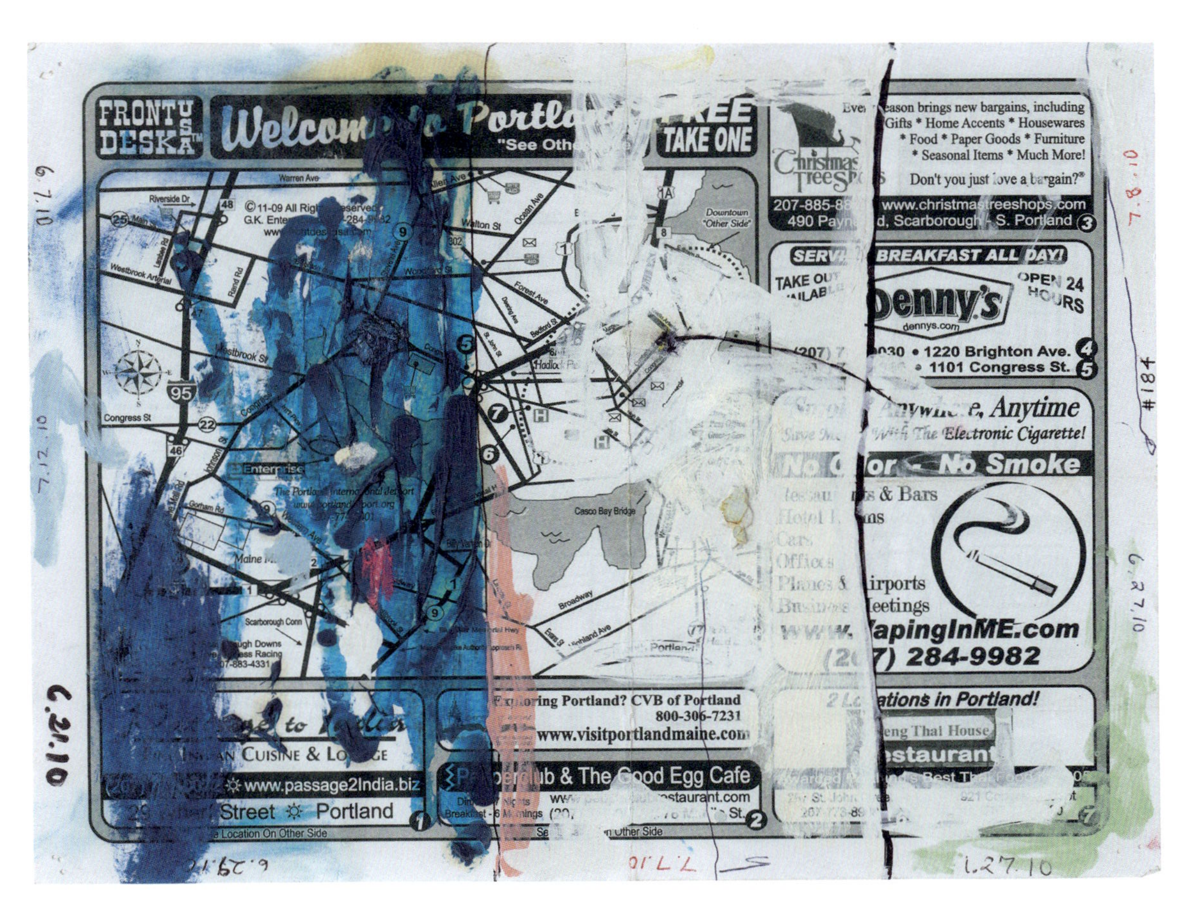
FRONT DESK USA Welcome to Portland
"See Othe
FREE TAKE ONE
Warren Ave
Riverside Dr
©11-09 All Rights Reserved
G.K. Enter
www
Westbrook Arterial
Rand Rd
Walton St
Ocean Ave
Westbrook St
95
Congress St
Enterprise
The Portland International Jetport
www.portlandjetport.org
07-883-4331
Maine M
Scarborough Conn
ugh Downs
ness Racing
Forest Ave
Bedford St
St. John St
Casco Bay Bridge
Broadway
Eastern
Highland Ave
Exploring Portland? CVB of Portland
800-306-7231
www.visitportlandmaine.com
to India
INDIAN CUISINE & LOUNGE
www.passage2India.biz
Street ☀ Portland
Location On Other Side
Paperclub & The Good Egg Cafe
restaurant.com
Even season brings new bargains, including
Gifts * Home Accents * Housewares
* Food * Paper Goods * Furniture
* Seasonal Items * Much More!
Don't you just love a bargain?®
207-885-88
490 Payn
www.christmastreeshops.com
d. Scarborough - S. Portland
Christmas Tree Shops
SERV
TAKE OU
AILABLE
BREAKFAST ALL DAY!
OPEN 24 HOURS
Denny's
dennys.com
(207)
030 • 1220 Brighton Ave.
• 1101 Congress St.
Anywhere, Anytime
Save Money With The Electronic Cigarette!
No Odor - No Smoke
Restaurants & Bars
Hotel Rooms
Cars
Offices
Planes & Airports
Business Meetings
www.VapingInME.com
(207) 284-9982
2 Locations in Portland!
eng Thai House
Restaurant

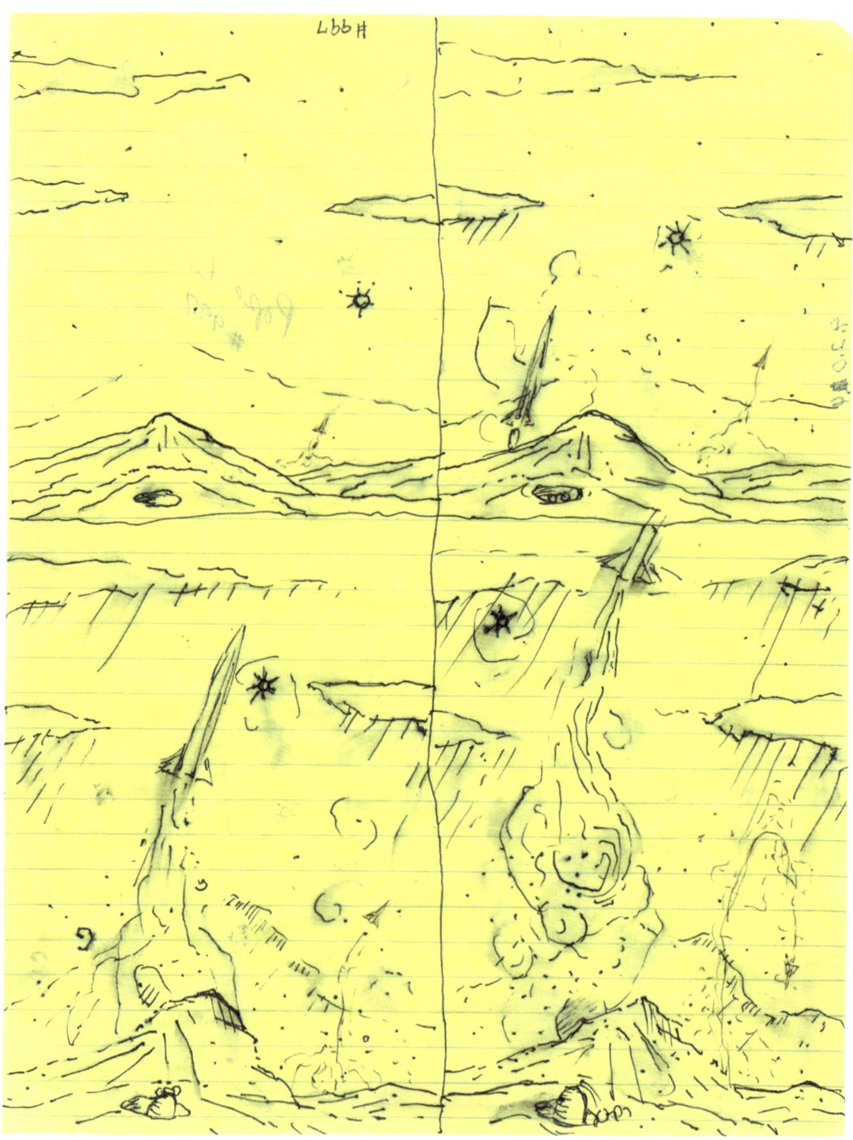

Pope.L, *Failure Drawing #997 Four Scenes*, 2004

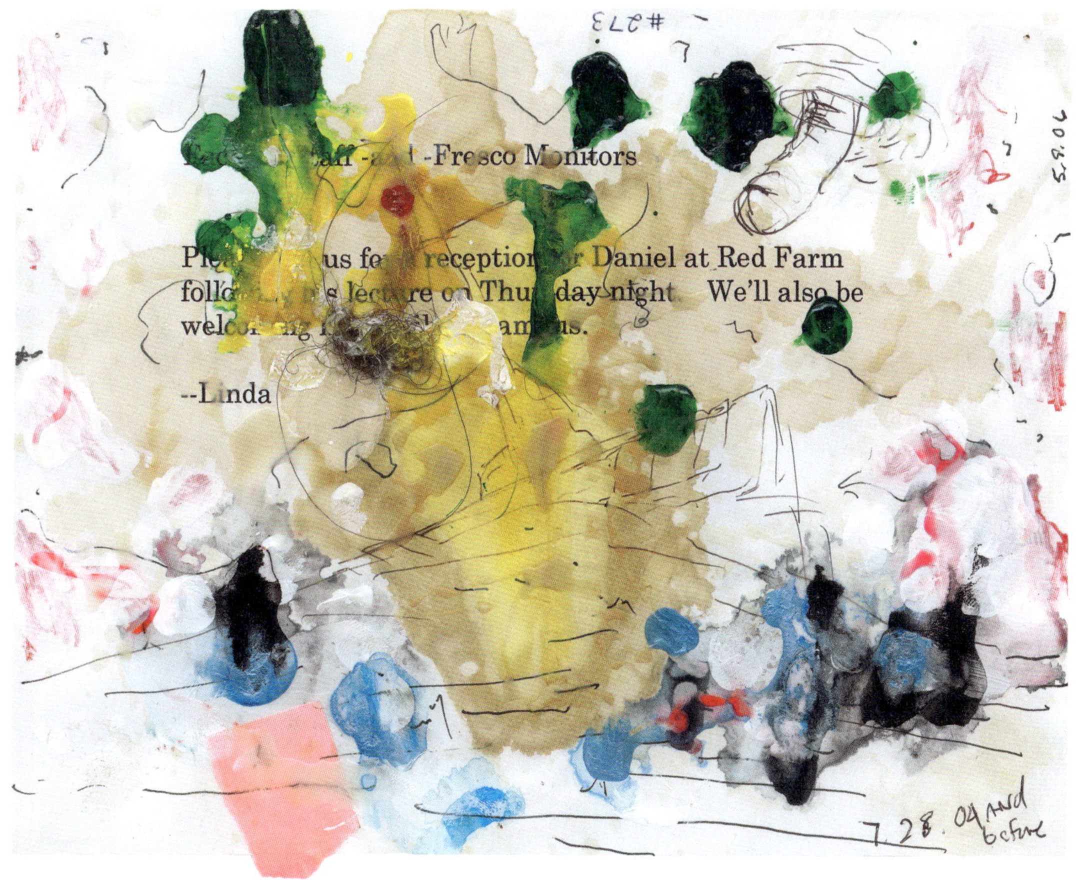

Pope.L, *Failure Drawing #273 Fresco Monitors Yellow, green, blue coffee*, 2004–2006

Pope.L, Failure Drawing #110 Rocket Fumble, Yellow, Green, Blue Sky, 2004–2006

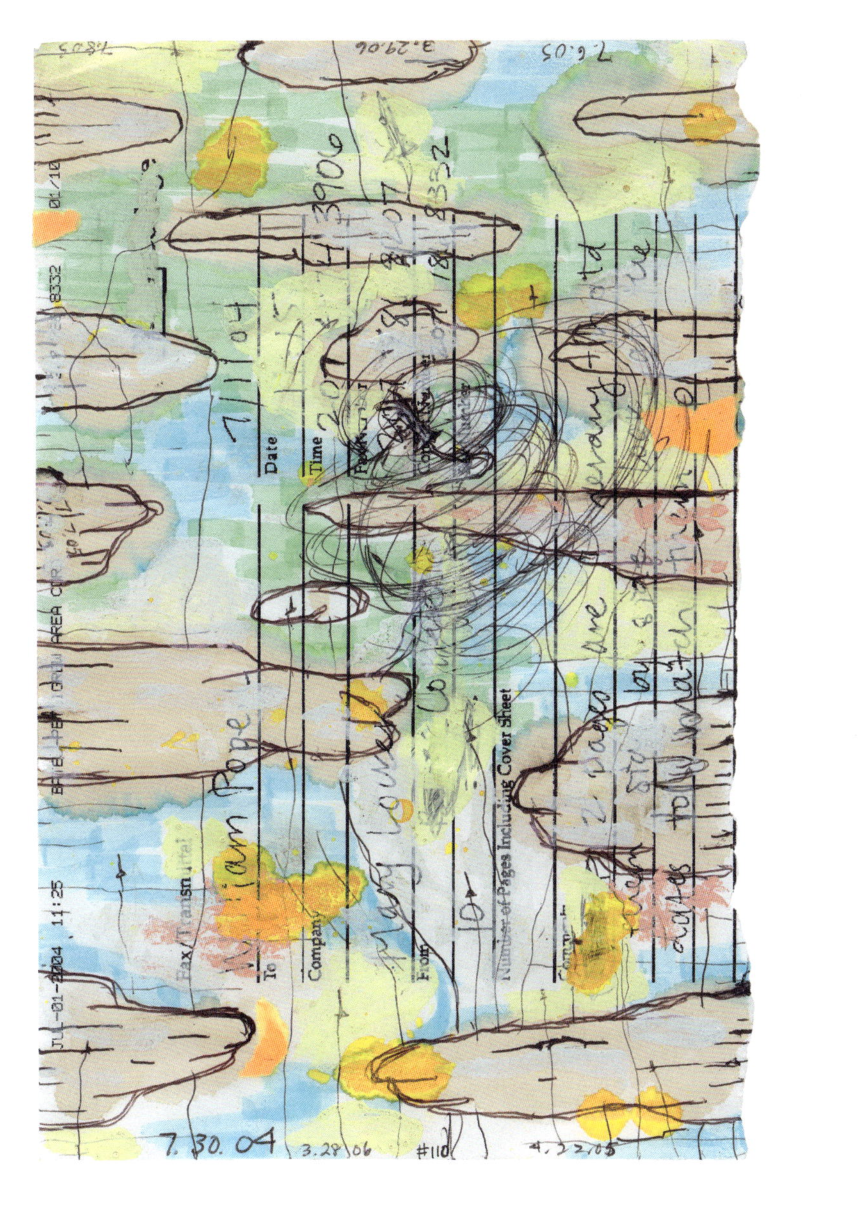

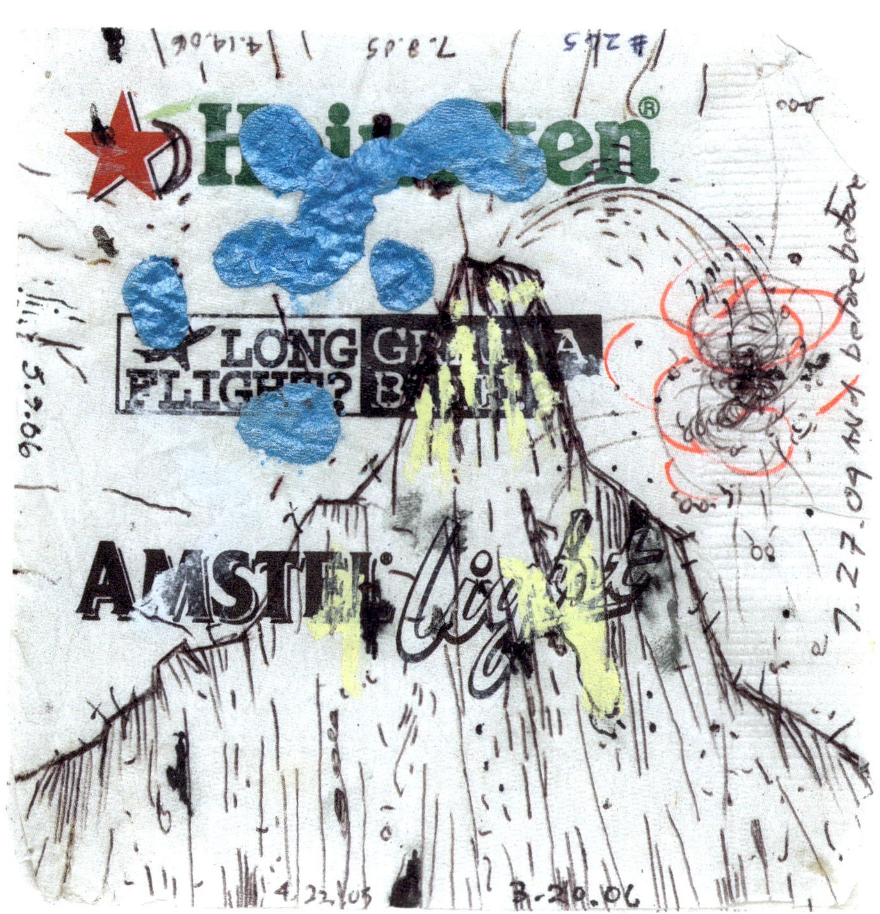

Pope.L, *Failure Drawing #265 Disaster Off Beer Mountain*, 2004–2006

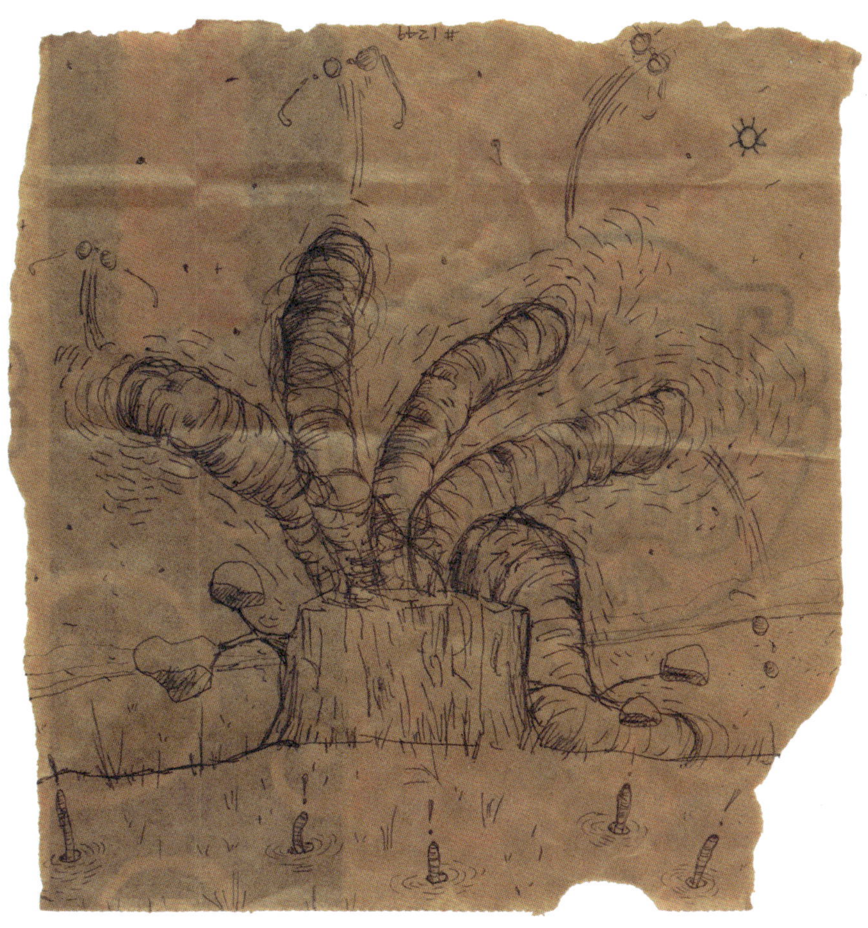

Pope.L, *Failure Drawing #1249 Stump, Albany, NY, My Birthday. The End of the World*, 2004

Pope.L, *Failure Drawing #127 I Have This Fear…*, 2004

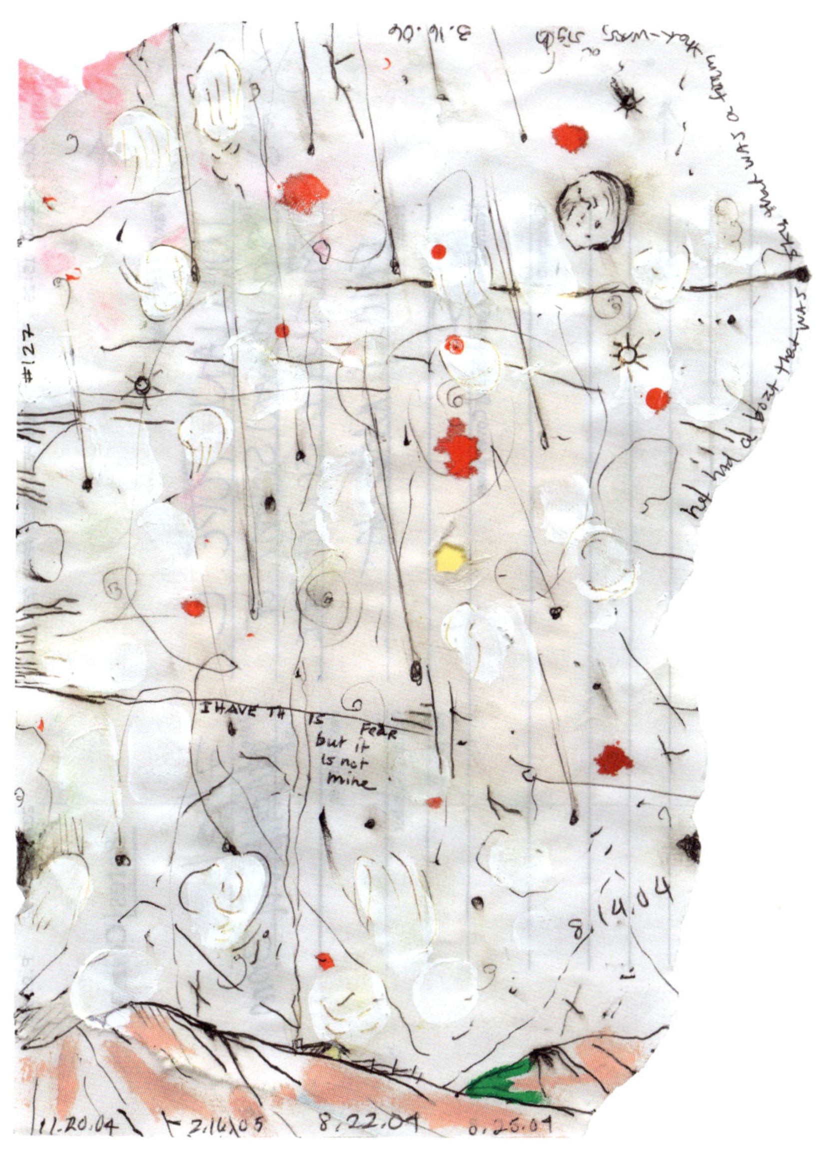
#127
I HAVE TH IS FEAR
but it
is not
mine
8.14.04
3.16.06
11.20.04   2.16\05   8.22.04   0.25.04

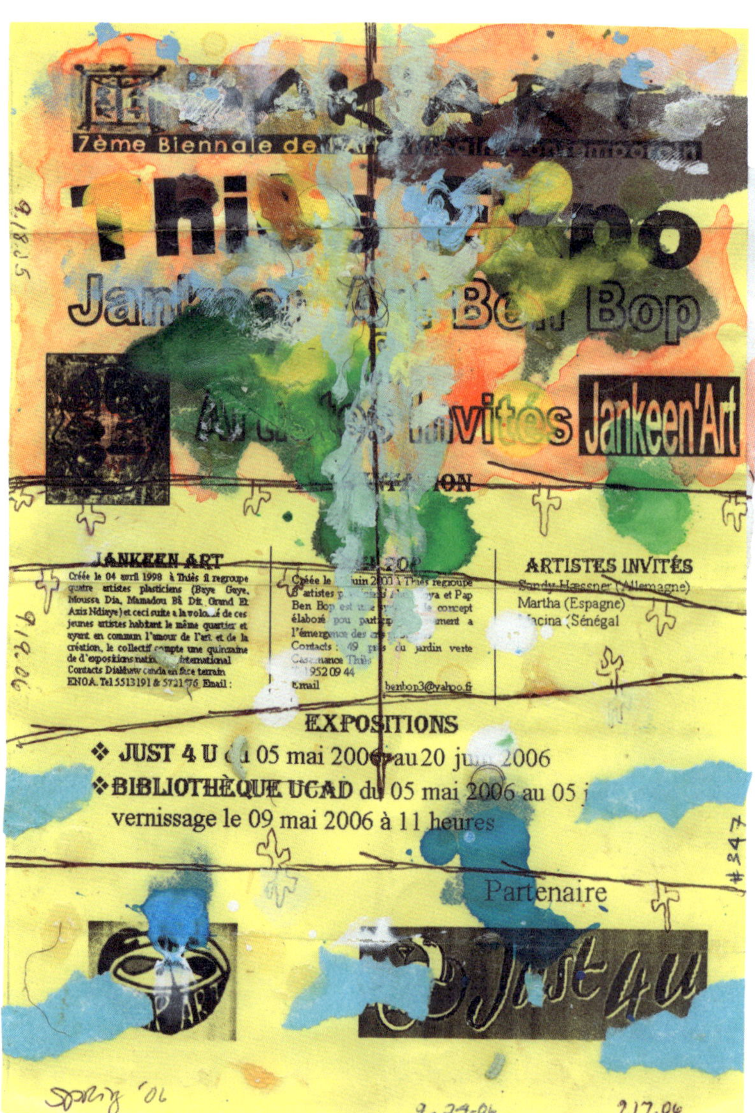

Pope.L, *Failure Drawing #347 Jankeen Art Reversible Cacti, 2005–2006*

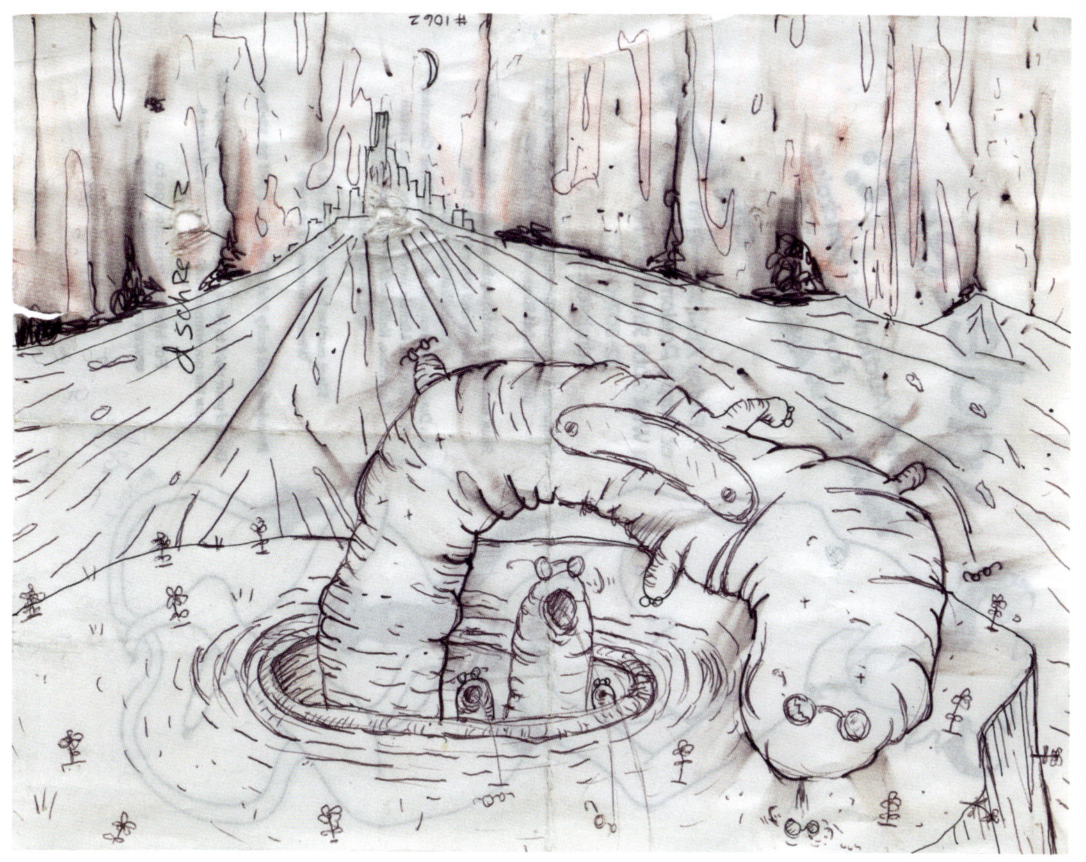

Pope.L, *Failure Drawing #1062 Near the City*, 2004

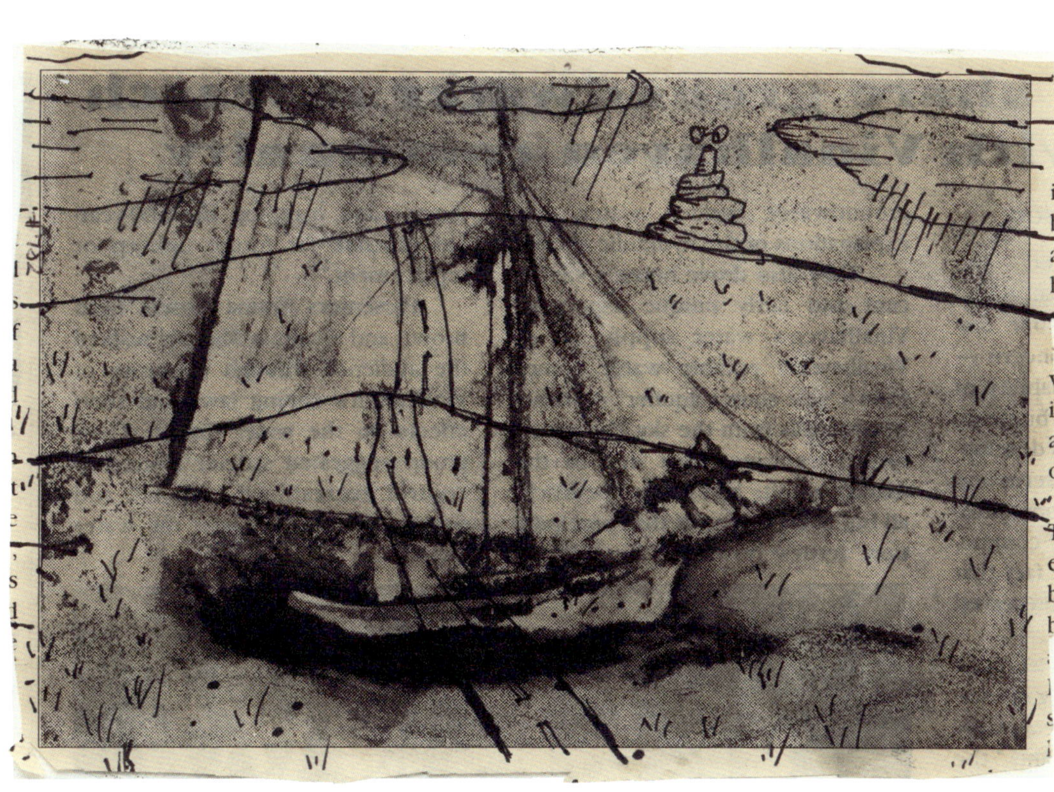

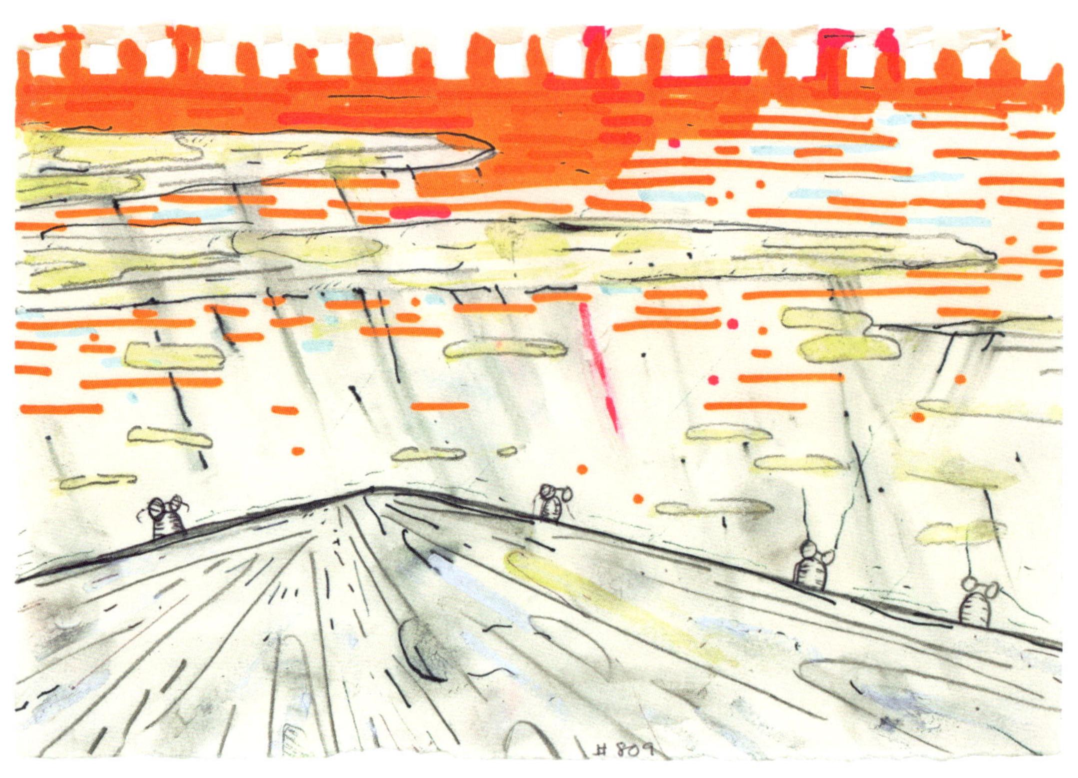

Pope.L, *Failure Drawing #809 Communicating With the Mourning*, 2004

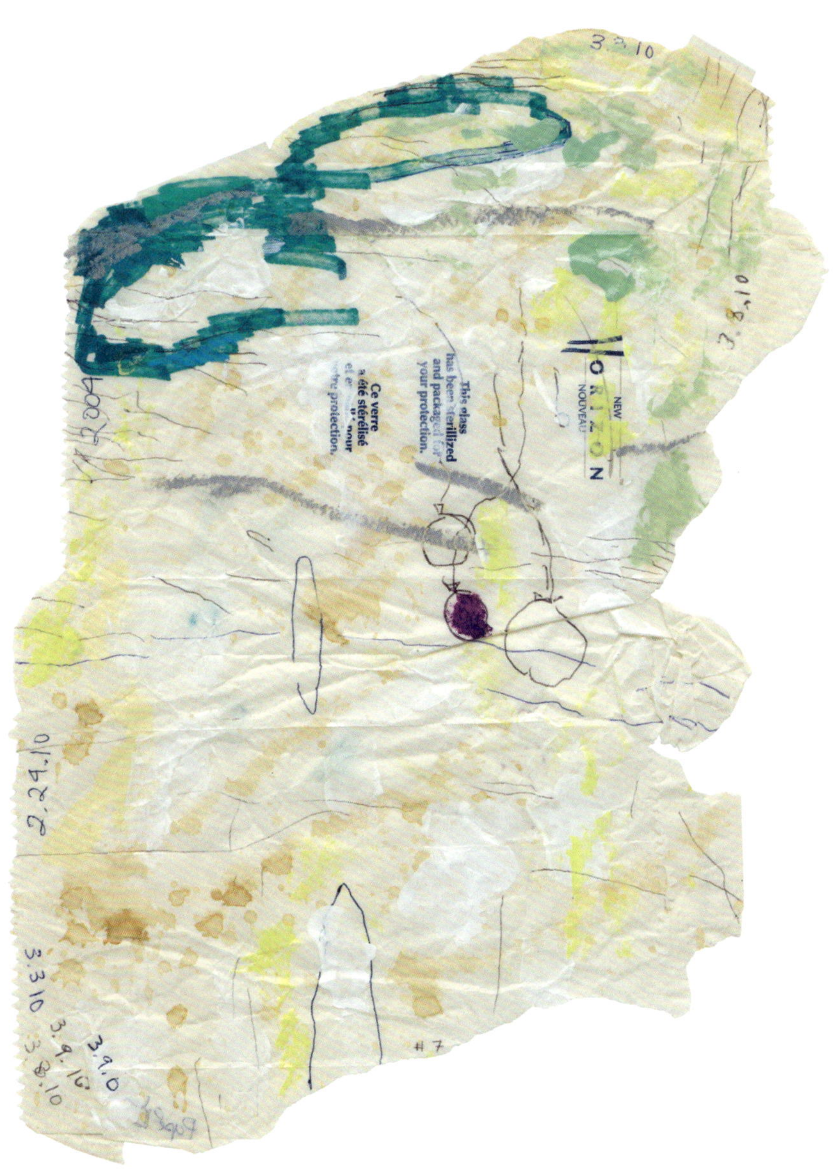

Pope.L, *Failure Drawing #7*, 2007

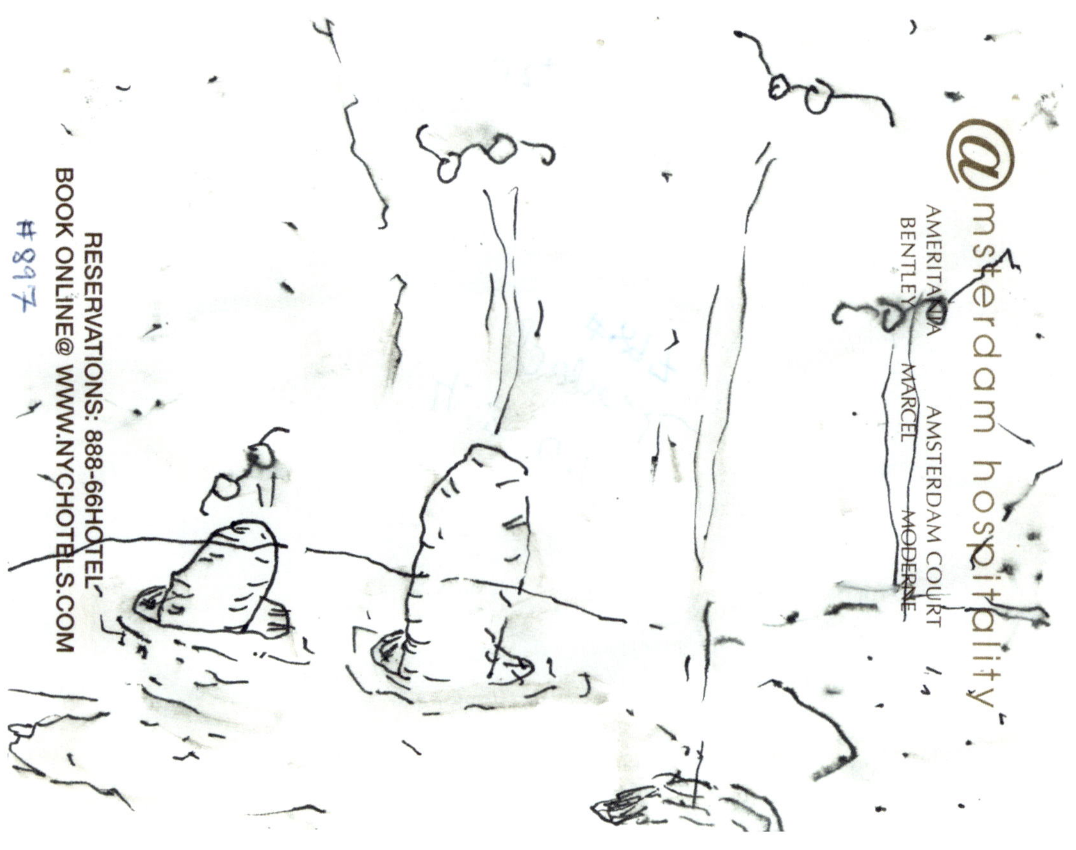

Pope.L, *Failure Drawing #897 Creatures Calling their glasses (soft rocket vision)*, 2004

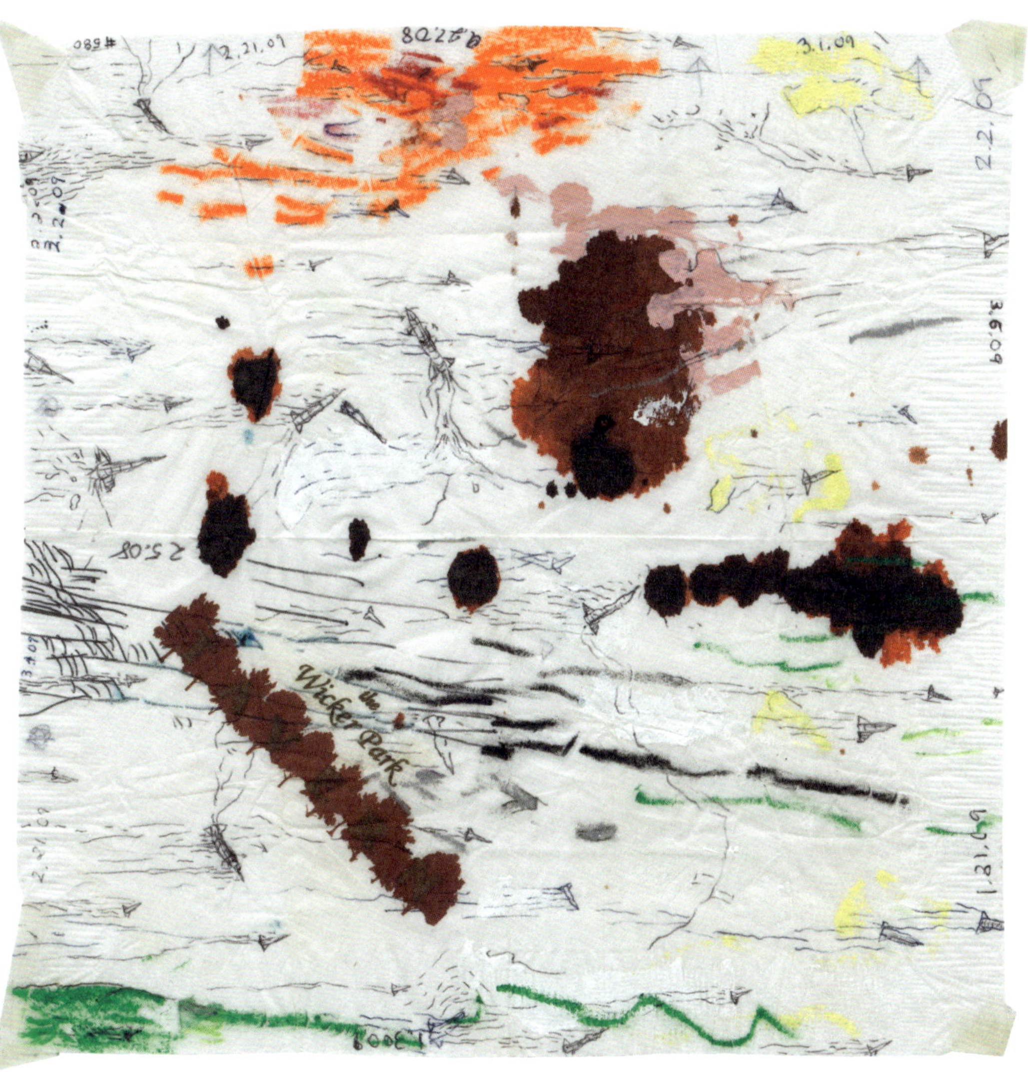

Pope.L, *Failure Drawing #580*, 2004–2007

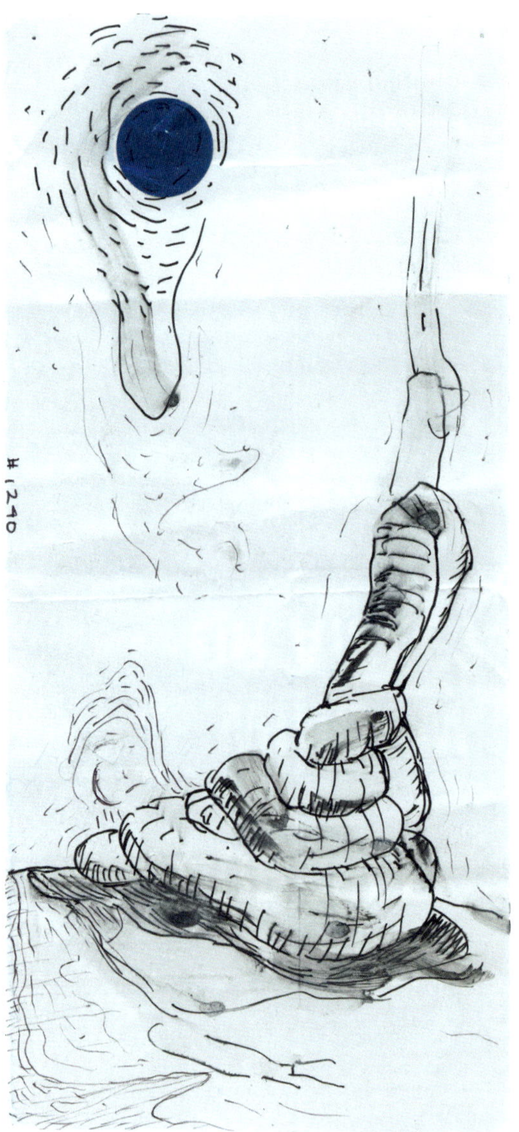

Pope.L, *Failure Drawing #1240 Blue Sun, Best Western Dining Room*, 2004

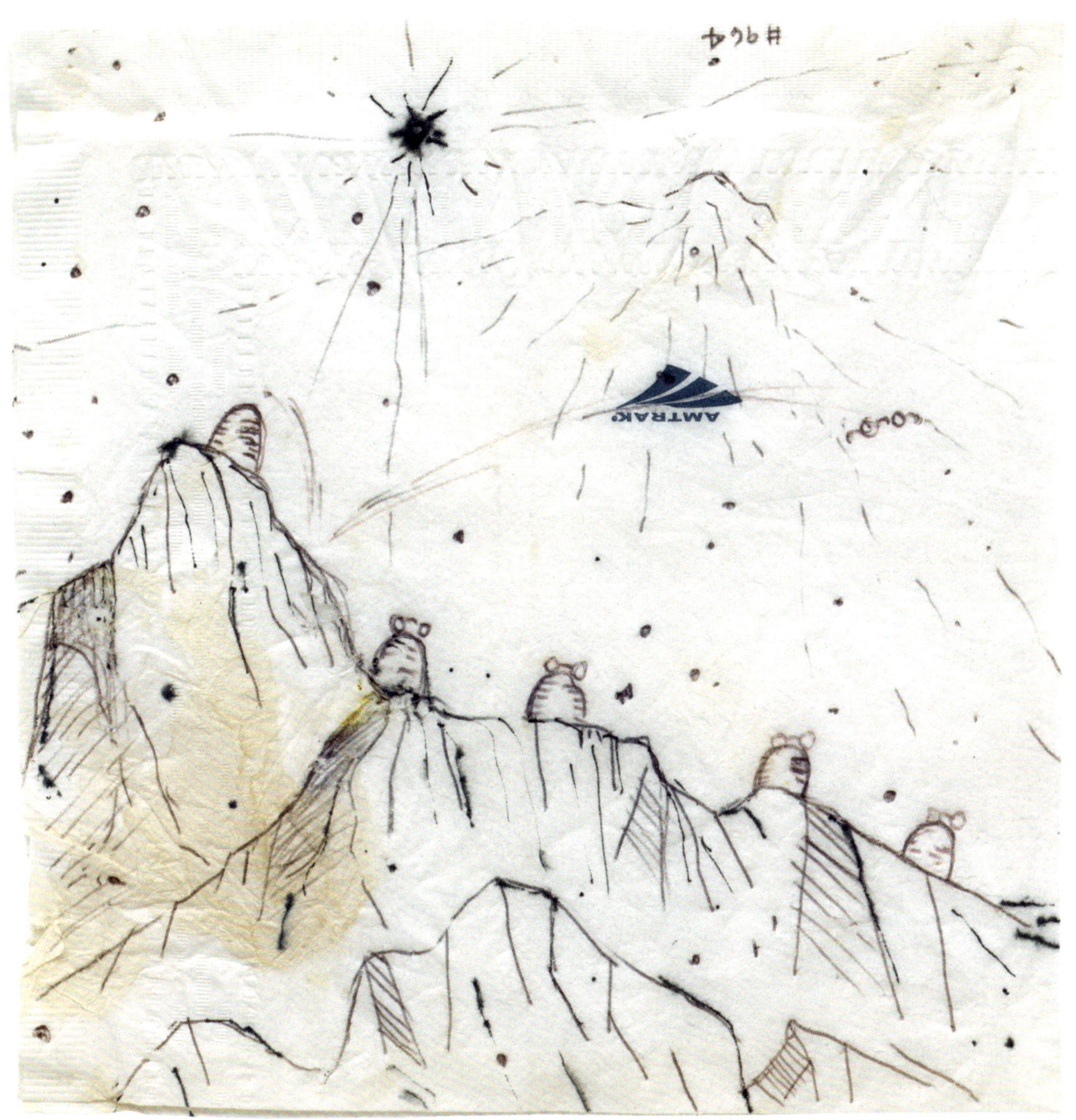

Pope.L, *Failure Drawing #964 Looking Back at the Sun*, 2004

Pope.L, *Failure Drawing #33 Red Cloud*, 2004–2006

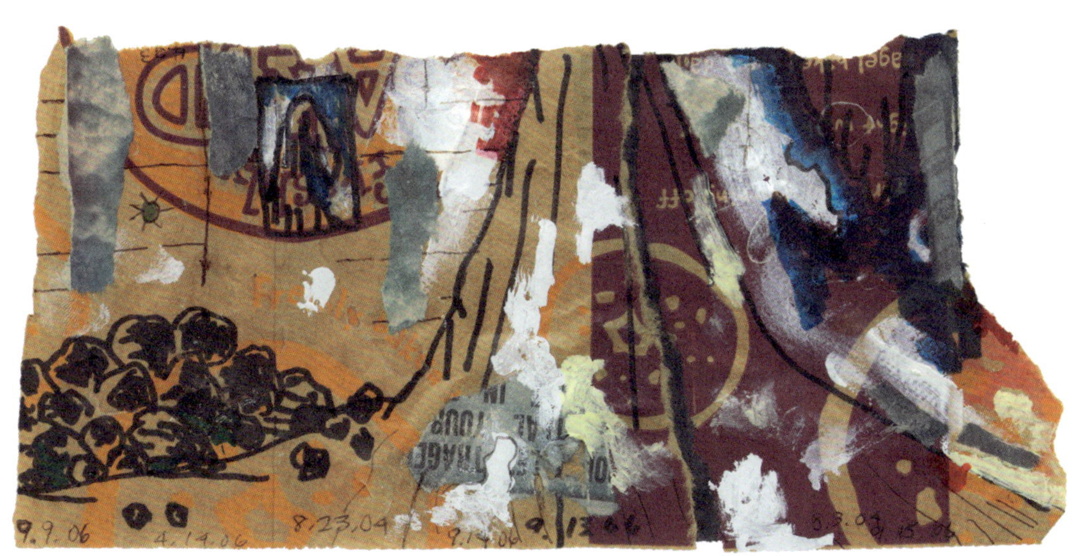

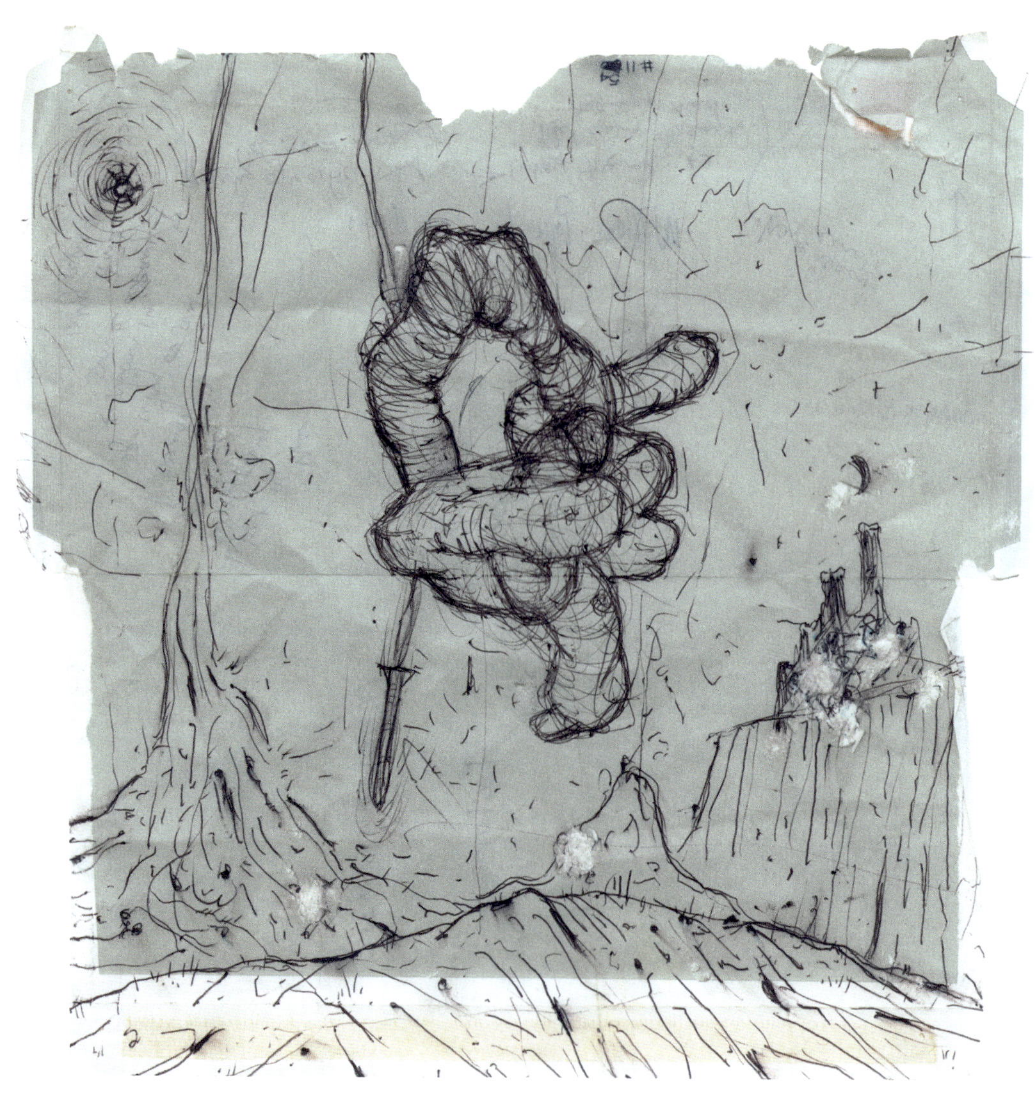

Pope.L, *Failure Drawing #1154 Rocket Cluster Grey*, 2004

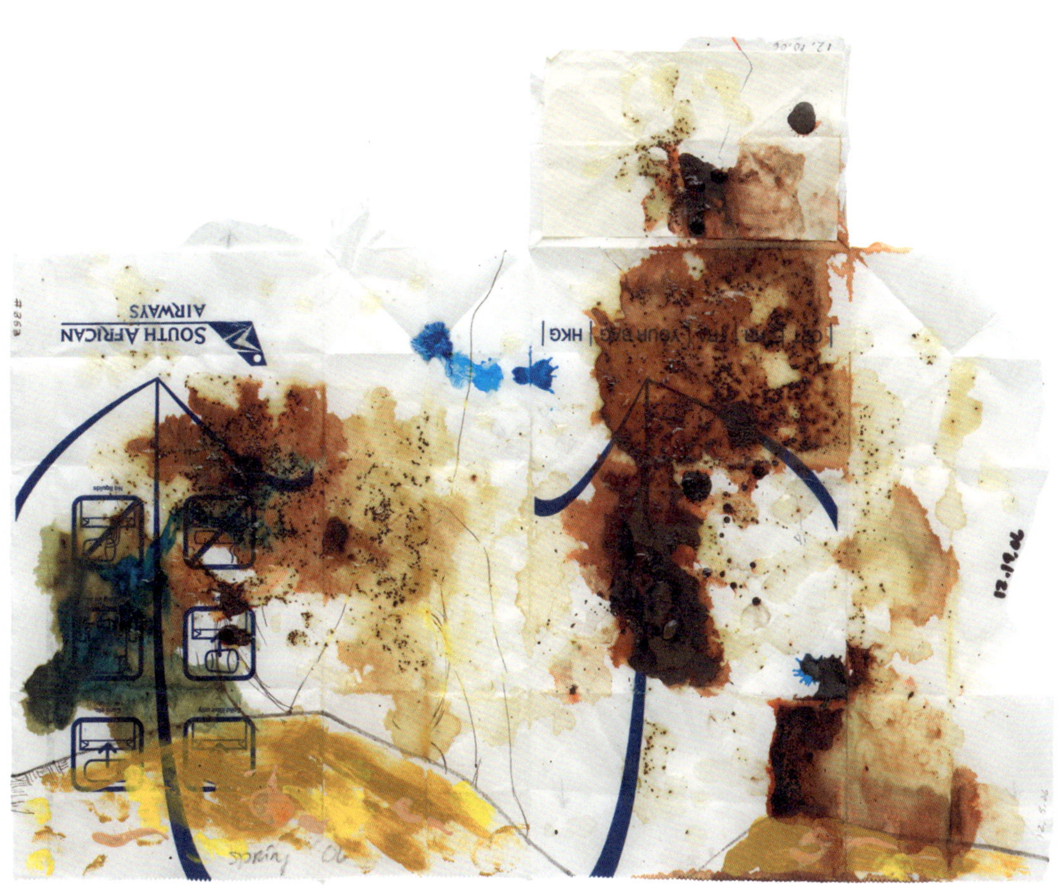

Pope.L, *Failure Drawing #353 Real Landscape*, 2006

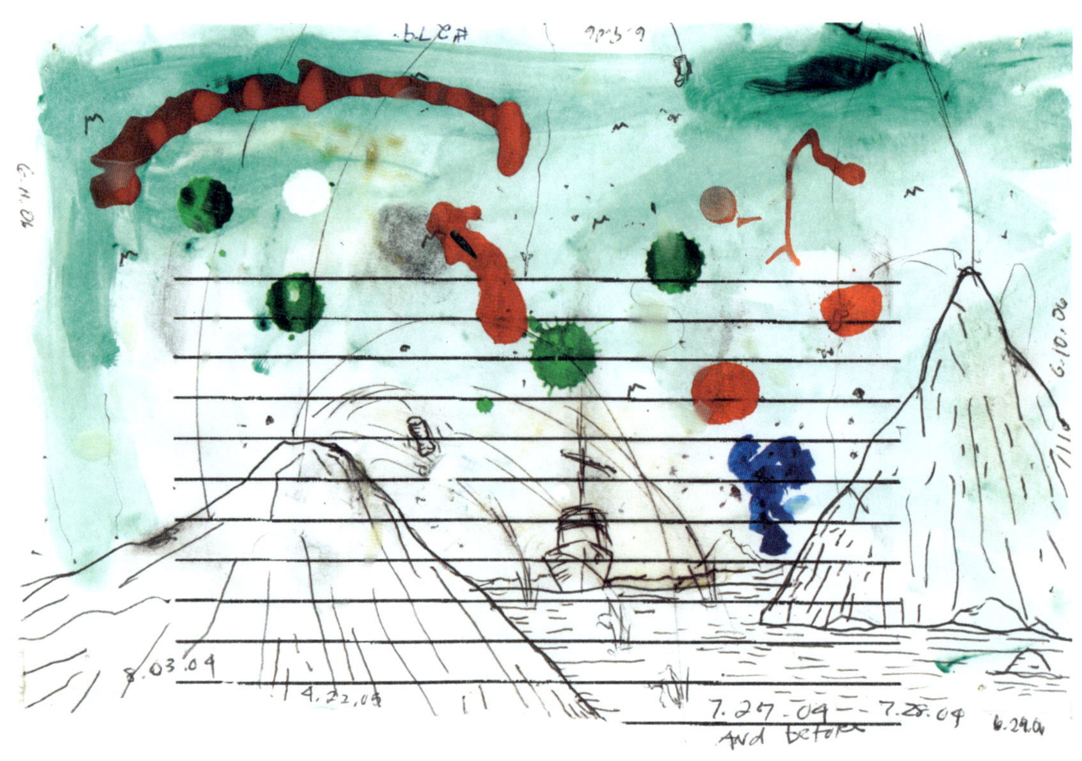

Pope.L, *Failure Drawing #279 Everything Falls, Green Sky*, 2004–2006

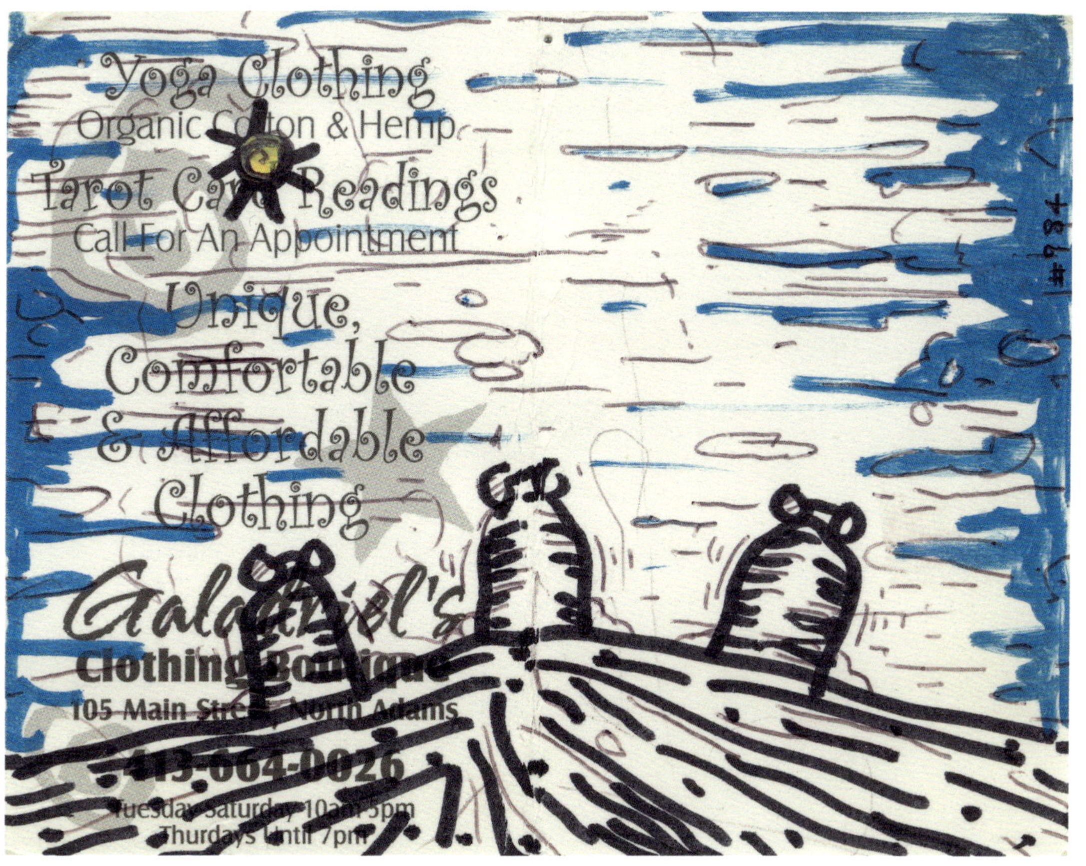

Pope.L, *Failure Drawing #984 Three Worms Yoga Advert*, 2004

Pope.L, *Failure Drawing #1026 Rocket falling, Carrot and Melon*, 2004

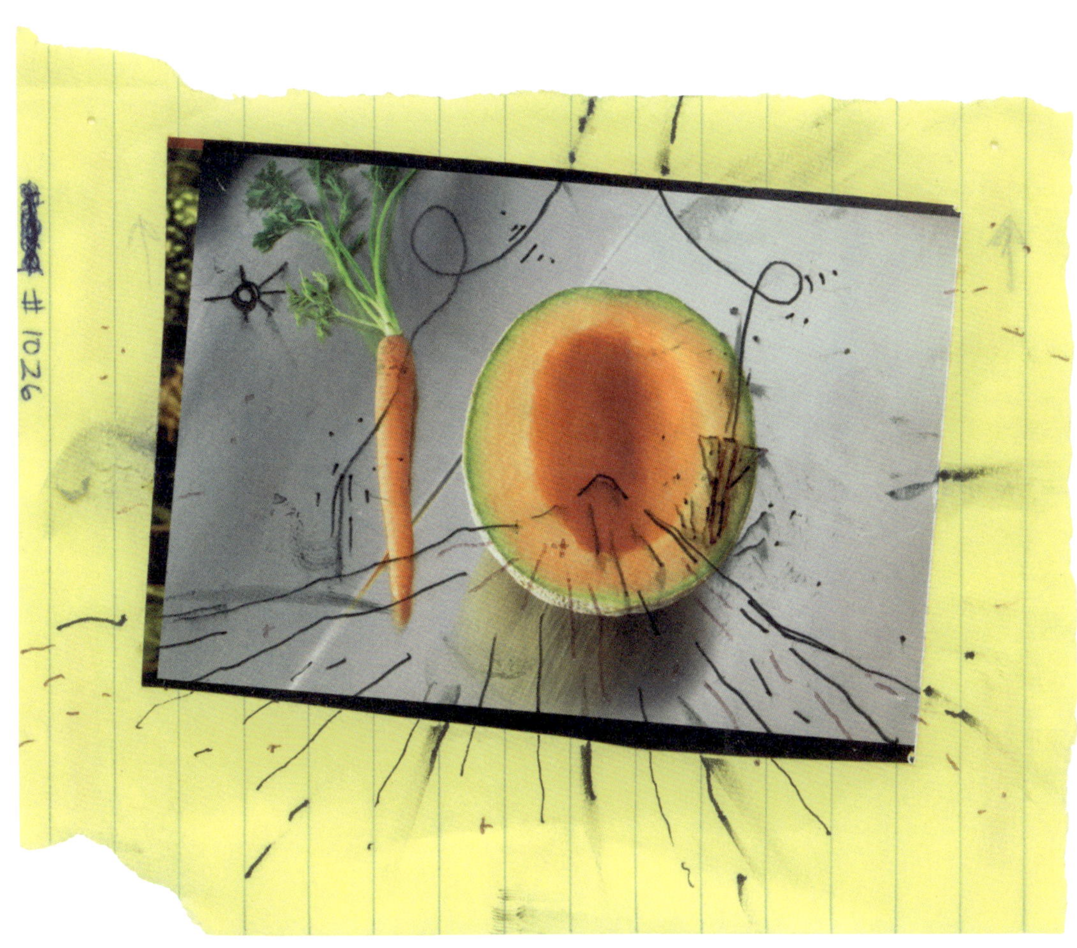

1026

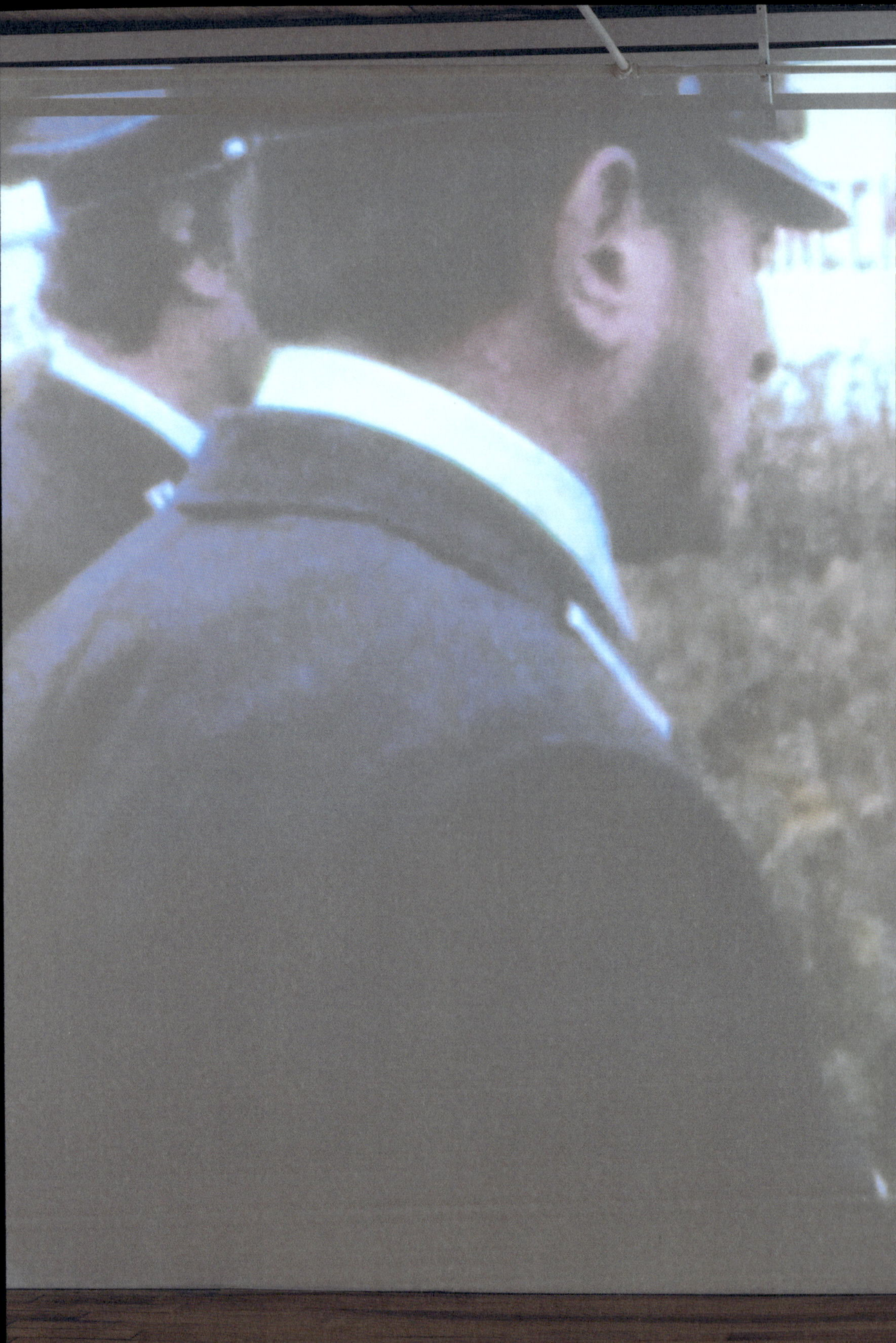

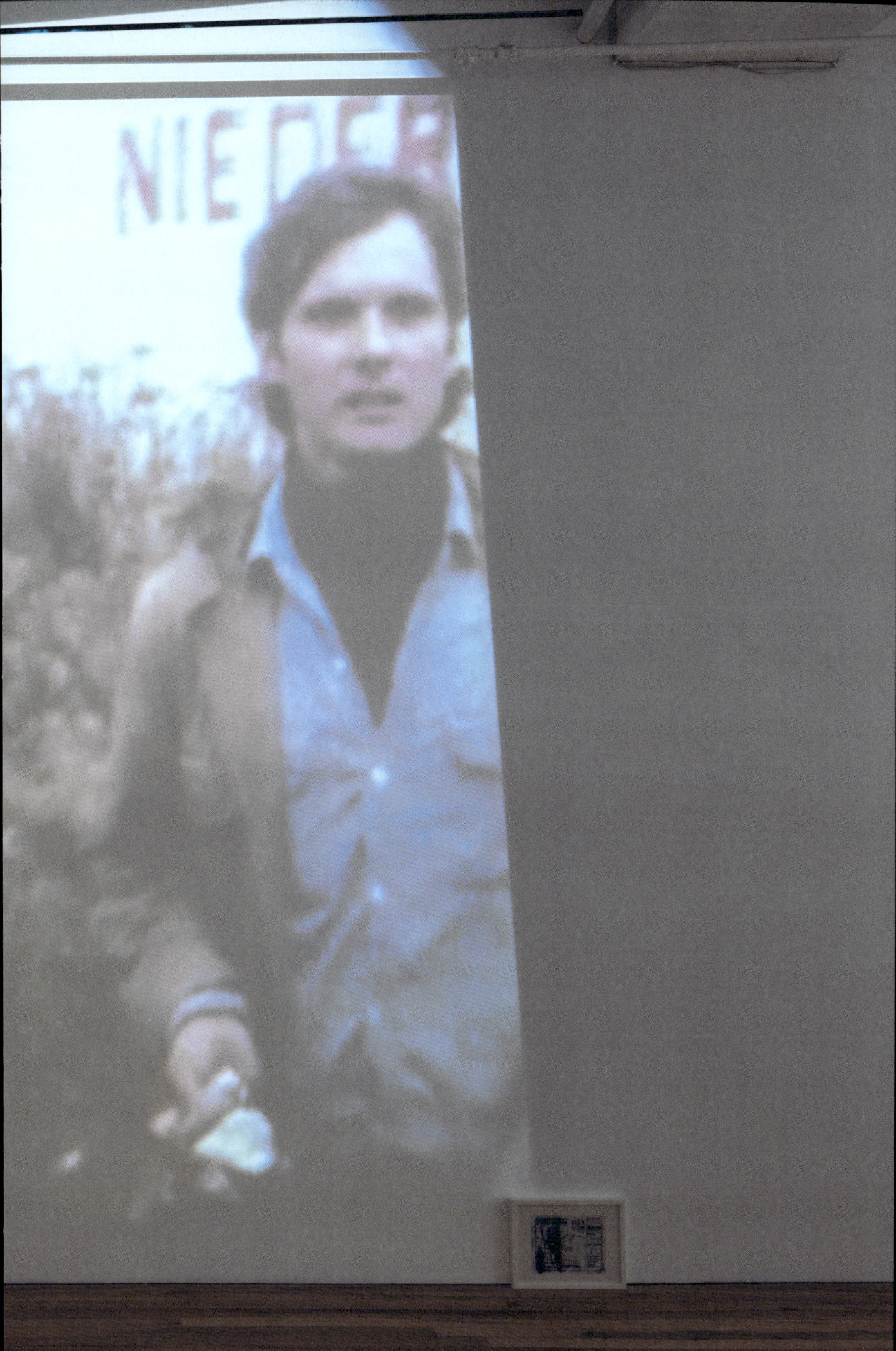
NIE DER

Pages 94–97
Gordon Matta-Clark, *The Wall*, 1976/2007

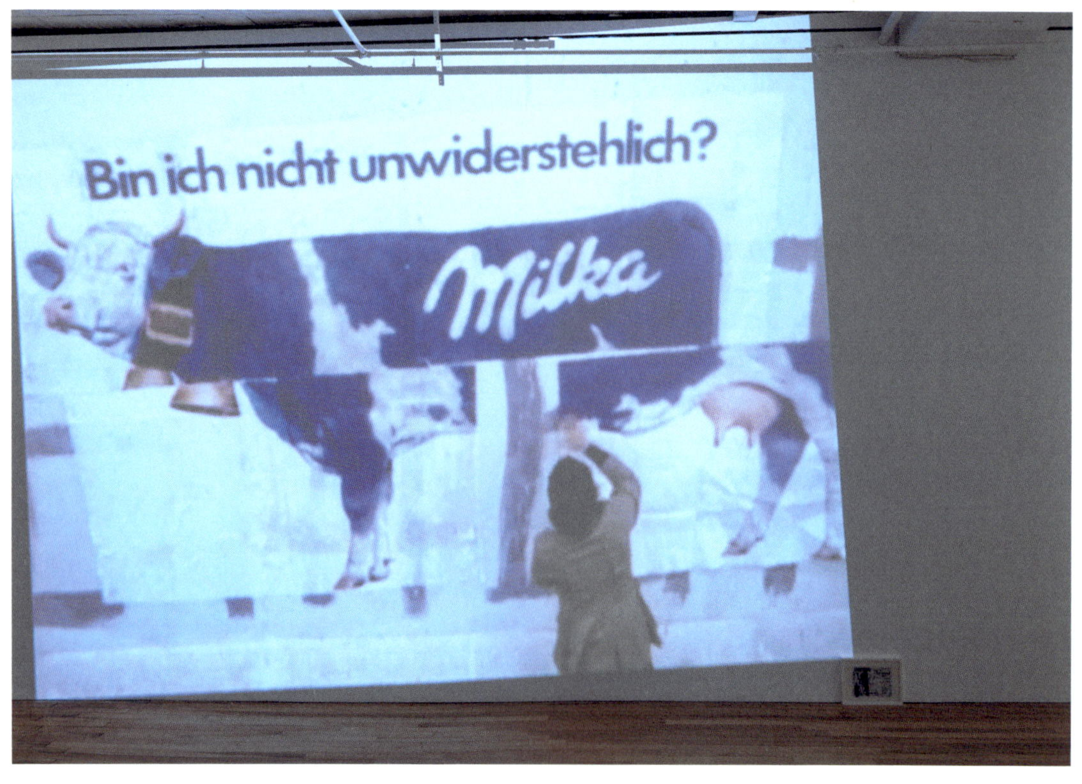

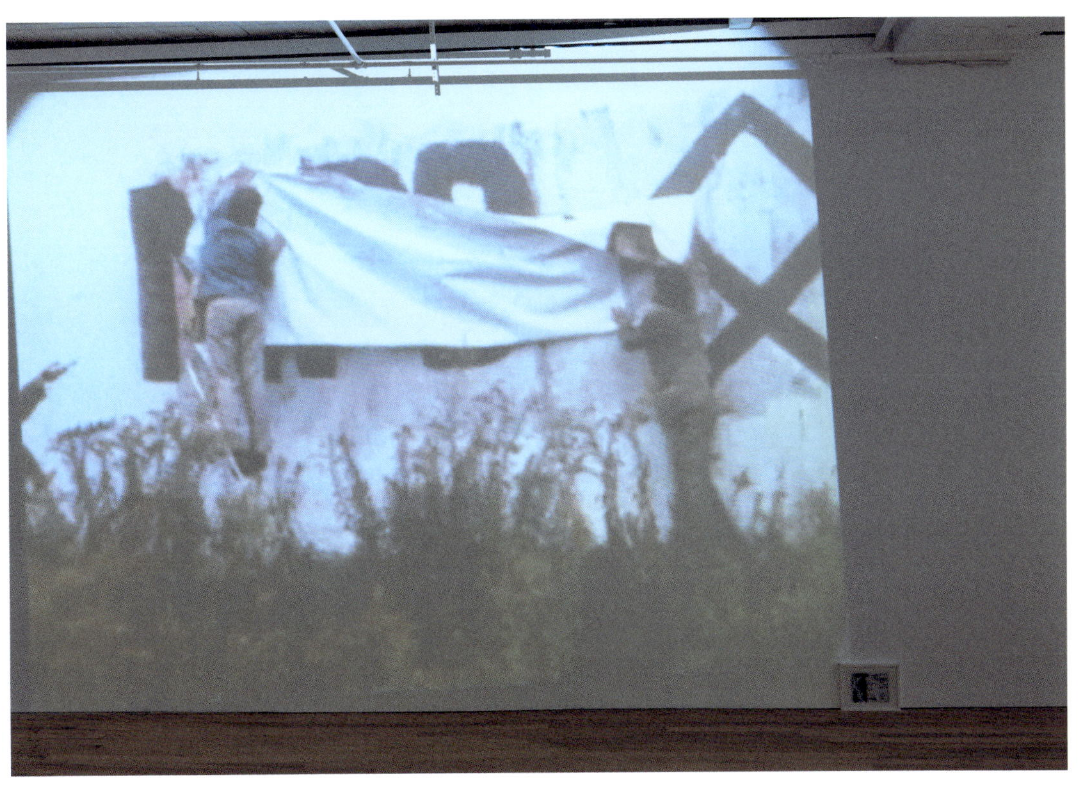

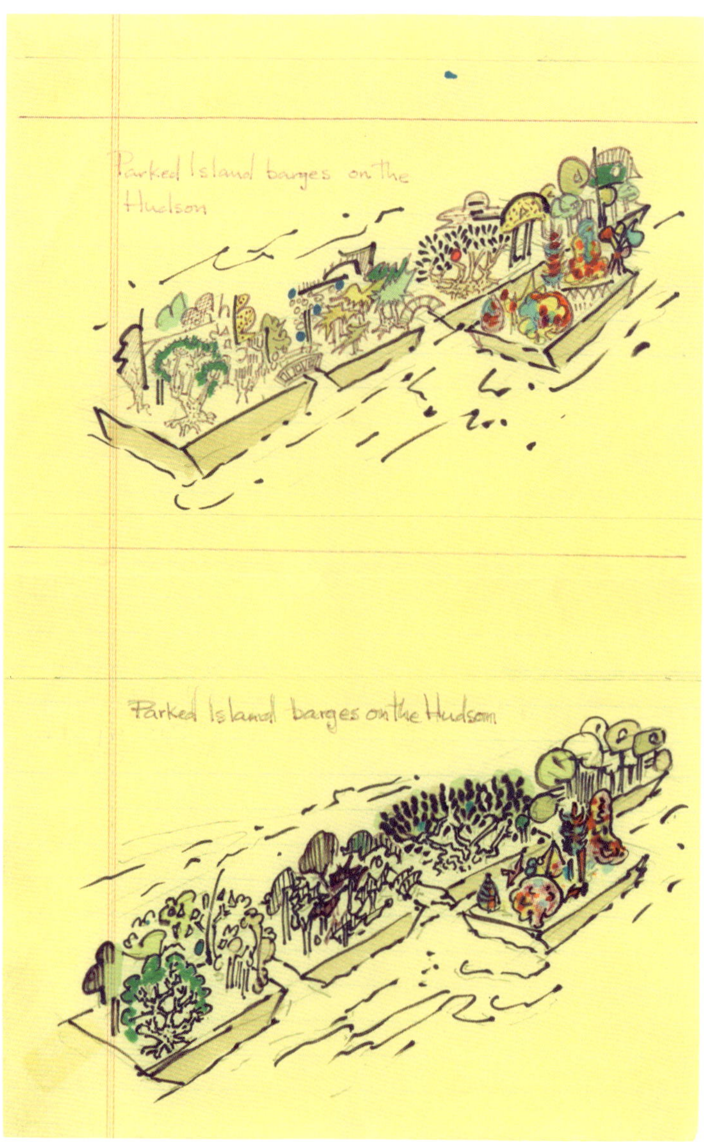

Gordon Matta-Clark, *Parked Island Barges on the Hudson*, 1970–1971

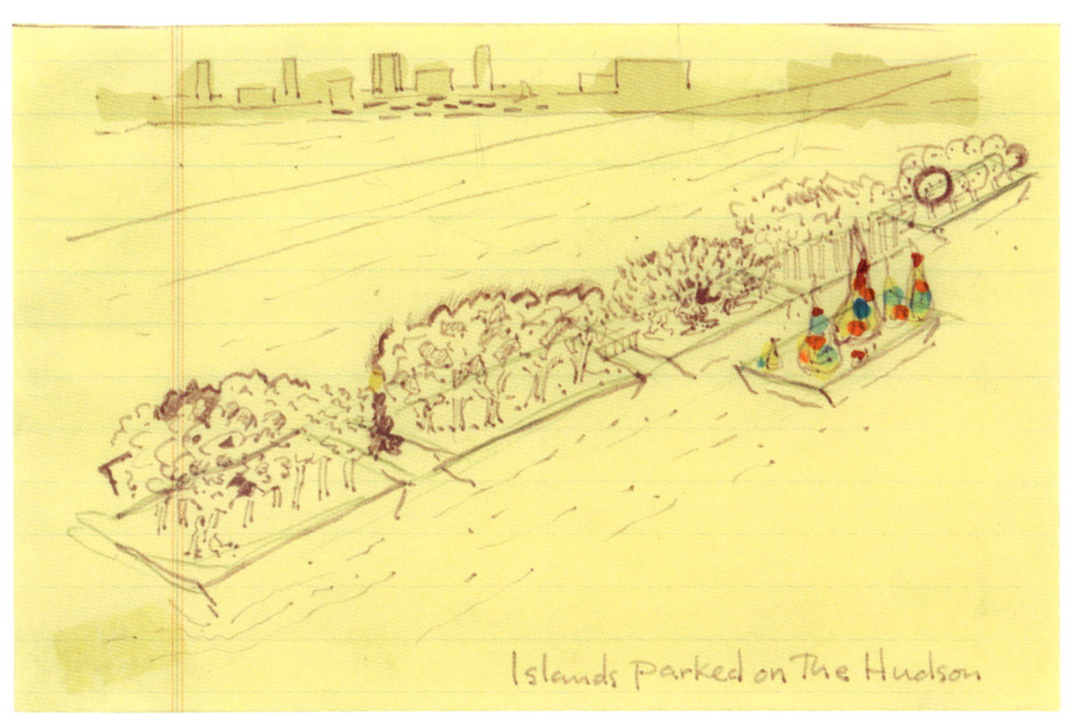

Gordon Matta-Clark, *Islands Parked on the Hudson*, 1970–1971

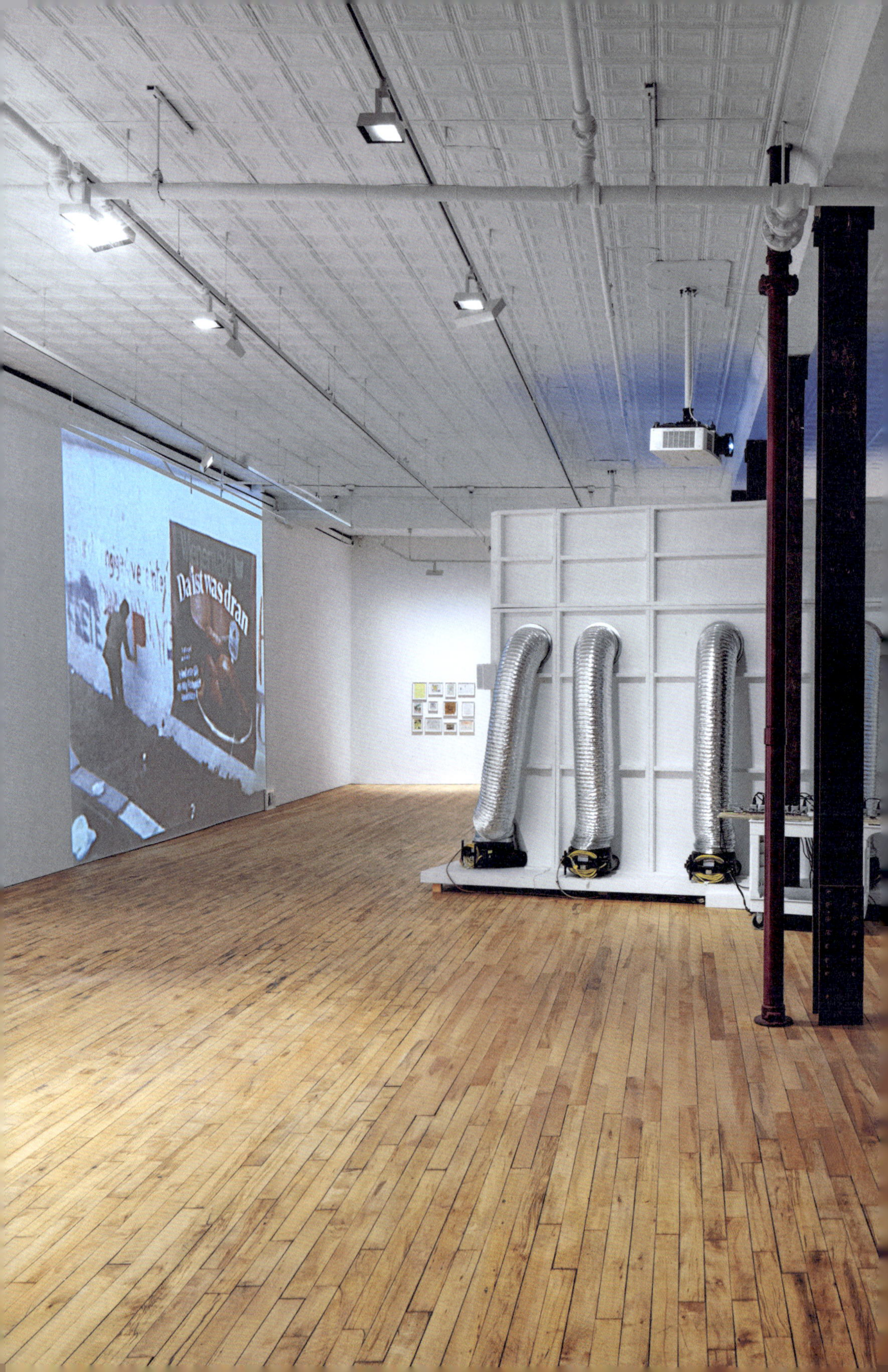

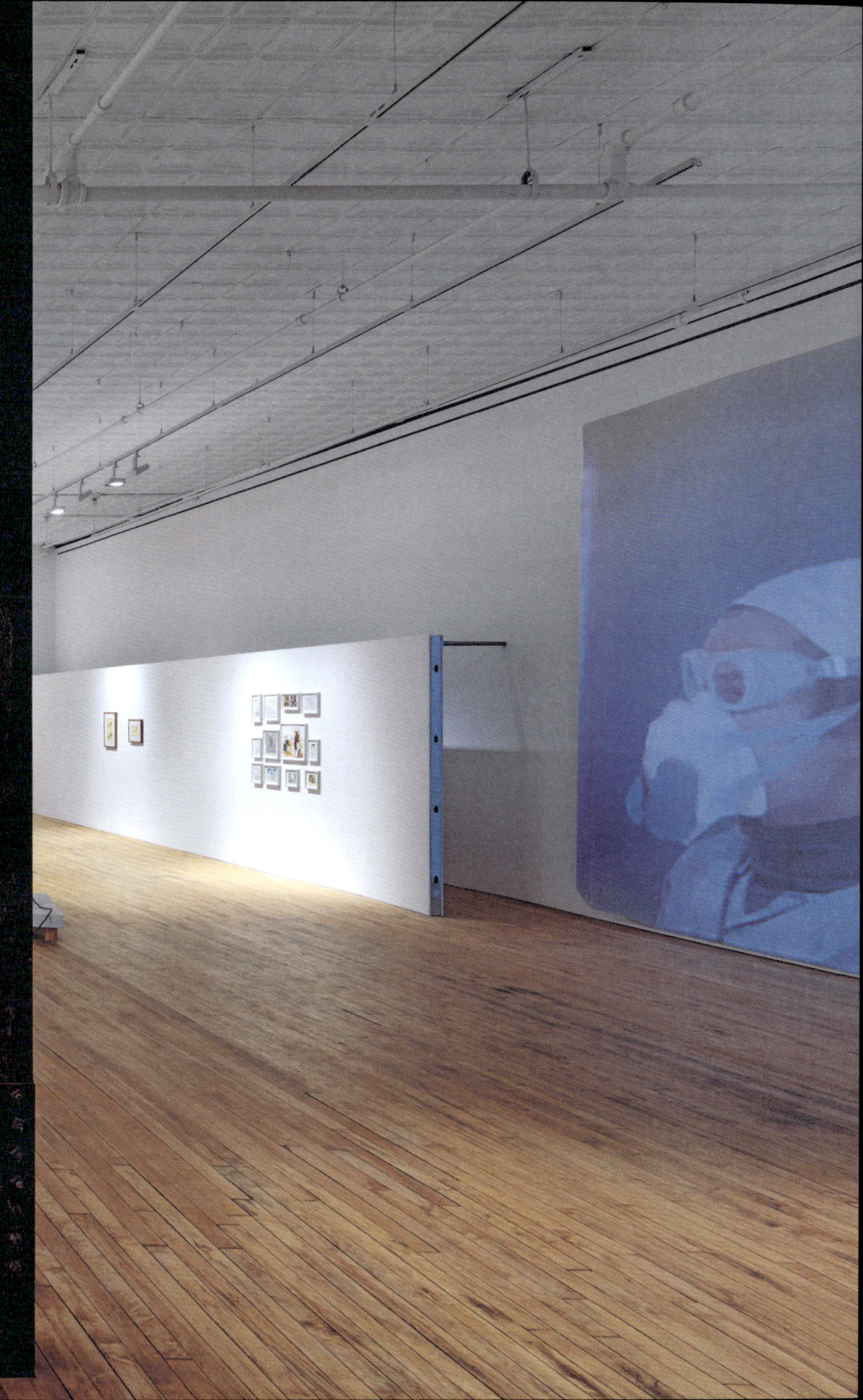

Works by Gordon Matta-Clark

Bingo X Ninths, 1974
16mm film, 9:40 min., color, silent
Overall dimensions variable
Pages 48–51

Conical Intersect, 1975
16mm film, 18:40 min., color, silent
Overall dimensions variable
Pages 52–53

Dragon Building, 1978
Ink on paper, two-sided
12 ⅜ × 7 ⅞ inches
31.5 × 20 cm
Estate of Gordon Matta-Clark
Page 38

Dragon Building, 1978
Ink on paper, two-sided
12 ⅜ × 7 ⅞ inches
31.5 × 20 cm
Estate of Gordon Matta-Clark
Page 39

Dragon Building, 1978
Ink on paper, two-sided
12 ⅜ × 7 ⅞ inches
31.5 × 20 cm
Estate of Gordon Matta-Clark
Page 41

Facade Theater Drop, 1974
Ink on paper
9 × 11 ¼ inches
22.9 × 28.6 cm
Estate of Gordon Matta-Clark
Page 31

Flag Pole Housing, 1974
Ink on paper
9 × 11 ¼ inches
22.9 × 28.6 cm
Estate of Gordon Matta-Clark
Page 35

Fresh Air Cart, 1974
Ink on paper
9 × 11 ¼ inches
22.9 × 28.6 cm
Estate of Gordon Matta-Clark
Page 37

High-Rise Excavation Diving Tower, 1974
Ink on paper
9 × 11 ¼ inches
22.9 × 28.6 cm
Estate of Gordon Matta-Clark
Page 34

Islands Parked on the Hudson, 1970–1971
Graphite and ink on paper
5 × 8 inches
12.7 × 20.3 cm
Estate of Gordon Matta-Clark
Page 99

A Marbled Mirrored Ball Room in the Way of the 2nd Avenue Subway, 1974
Ink on paper
9 × 11 ¼ inches
22.9 × 28.6 cm
Estate of Gordon Matta-Clark
Page 33

New York Subway Show Window Rocker, 1974
Ink on paper
9 × 11 ¼ inches
22.9 × 28.6 cm
Estate of Gordon Matta-Clark
Page 32

Parked Island Barges on the Hudson, 1970–1971
Graphite and ink on paper
12 ¼ × 8 inches
31.1 × 20.3 cm
Estate of Gordon Matta-Clark
Page 98

Untitled (Cut Drawing), 1973
Cut board and stucco
19 × 26 ⅝ × 1 inches
48.3 × 67.6 × 2.5 cm
Hort Family Collection
Page 45

The Wall, 1976/2007
Super-8 film, 15 min., color, sound
Music by Peter Gordon
Overall dimensions variable
Pages 94–97

A W-Hole House (Four Corners), 1973
Graphite and cardboard
26 ½ × 38 ¼ × 1 inches
67.3 × 97.2 × 2.5 cm
Estate of Gordon Matta-Clark
Page 47

Works by Pope.L

Dust Eater a.k.a. White Woman Eating A Donut, 2007–2009/2022
Video, 3:55 min. (loop), color, sound
Overall dimensions variable
Page 65

Failure Drawing #7, 2007
Acrylic, oil, Bic pen, pastel, coffee, and tape on paper
11 ¼ × 8 ⅜ inches
28.6 × 21.3 cm
Page 81

Failure Drawing #33 Red Cloud, 2004–2006
Ink, black marker, ballpoint pen, acrylic, stains, and
newspaper collage on joined brown paper
4 ⅝ × 9 ¾ inches
11.8 × 24.8 cm
Private collection
Page 87

Failure Drawing #107 The Night Laughs To See … , 2004–2006
Ink and acrylic on hotel stationery
5 ½ × 4 ¼ inches
14 × 10.8 cm
Not illustrated

Failure Drawing #110 Rocket Fumble, Yellow, Green, Blue Sky,
2004–2006
Ink, ballpoint pen, acrylic, highlighter, colored marker,
and collage on printed paper
8 ½ × 5 ⅝ inches
21.6 × 14.3 cm
Page 71

Failure Drawing #127 I Have This Fear … , 2004
Ballpoint pen, acrylic, tape, and yellow Post-it on paper
8 ½ × 6 ⅛ inches
21.6 × 15.6 cm
Collection of Sophie Hong
Page 75

Failure Drawing #184, 2004–2007
Acrylic, oil, ink, and graphite on printed paper
11 × 8 ⅜ inches
27.9 × 21.3 cm
Page 67

Failure Drawing #265 Disaster Off Beer Mountain, 2004–2006
Ink, ballpoint pen, and acrylic on napkin
5 × 5 inches
12.7 × 12.7 cm
Private collection
Page 72

Failure Drawing #273 Fresco Monitors Yellow, green, blue coffee,
2004–2006
Ink, acrylic, stains, hair, glue, and collage on
printed paper
6 ¾ × 8 ⅜ inches
17.1 × 21.3 cm
Page 69

Failure Drawing #279 Everything Falls, Green Sky, 2004–2006
Ink, ballpoint pen, acrylic, hair, and glue on
photocopy page
5 ¾ × 8 ½ inches
14.6 × 21.6 cm
Page 90

Failure Drawing #347 Jankeen Art Reversible Cacti, 2005–2006
Ink, ballpoint pen, acrylic, watercolor, hair, glue, and
collage on printed paper
8 ⅛ × 5 ¾ inches
20.6 × 14.6 cm
Page 76

Failure Drawing #353 Real Landscape, 2006
Ballpoint pen, acrylic, glue, coffee grinds, and stains on
printed paper
12 ¼ × 15 ¾ inches
31.1 × 40 cm
Page 89

Failure Drawing #357 Crashes in Crevice, 2006
Ink, acrylic, hair, and glue on printed paper
8 ¼ × 6 inches
21 × 15.2 cm
Not illustrated

Failure Drawing #391 Worm At Window, c. 2003–2008
Ballpoint pen on hotel stationery
7 ⅛ × 10 ⅜ inches
18.1 × 26.4 cm
Not illustrated

Failure Drawing #580, 2004–2007
Acrylic, oil, and graphite on napkin
10 × 10 inches
25.4 × 25.4 cm
Page 83

Failure Drawing #702 Mountain With Fence on Right, 2004
Ballpoint pen and ink on newsprint on paper
4 ⅜ × 6 ½ inches
11.1 × 16.5 cm
Private collection
Page 79

Failure Drawing #809 Communicating With the Mourning, 2004
Graphite, ink, ballpoint pen, colored marker, and acrylic
on paper
6 ⅛ × 9 inches
15.6 × 22.9 cm
Page 80

Failure Drawing #897 Creatures Calling their glasses (soft rocket vision), 2004
Ink on hotel stationery
4 ¼ × 5 ½ inches
10.8 × 14 cm
Page 82

Failure Drawing #898 Rockets Having Fallen, Worm Holes, 2004
Ink on hotel stationery
5 ½ × 4 ⅛ inches
14 × 10.5 cm
Not illustrated

Failure Drawing #945 Two Spectacles, 2004
Ballpoint pen, ink, and acrylic on printed paper
5 ½ × 8 ½ inches
14 × 21.6 cm
Not illustrated

Failure Drawing #964 Looking Back at the Sun, 2004
Ink, ballpoint pen, and stains on napkin
8 ¼ × 8 ¼ inches
21 × 21 cm
Page 85

Failure Drawing #984 Three Worms Yoga Advert, 2004
Ballpoint pen, black marker, and colored marker on printed card
4 ¼ × 5 ⅜ inches
10.8 × 13.7 cm
Page 91

Failure Drawing #997 Four Scenes, 2004
Ink and ballpoint pen on ruled paper
11 × 8 ½ inches
27.9 × 21.6 cm
Page 68

Failure Drawing #1026 Rocket falling, Carrot and Melon, 2004
Ink and cut magazine paper collage on ruled paper
4 ¾ × 5 ⅝ inches
12.1 × 14.3 cm
Collection of Martin and Rebecca Eisenberg
Page 93

Failure Drawing #1033 Creature Communication, 2004
Ballpoint pen and ink on hotel stationery
5 ½ × 4 ¼ inches
14 × 10.8 cm
Not illustrated

Failure Drawing #1062 Near the City, 2004
Ink and ballpoint pen on verso-printed paper
8 ⅜ × 11 inches
21.3 × 27.9 cm
Page 77

Failure Drawing #1154 Rocket Cluster Grey, 2004
Ink and ballpoint pen on verso-printed paper
9 ⅞ × 9 ¾ inches
25.1 × 24.8 cm
Private collection
Page 88

Failure Drawing #1240 Blue Sun, Best Western Dining Room, 2004
Ballpoint pen, ink, and collage on paper
8 ½ × 3 ⅞ inches
21.6 × 9.8 cm
Page 84

Failure Drawing #1249 Stump, Albany, NY, My Birthday. The End of the World, 2004
Ballpoint pen on brown paper
9 ¼ × 9 inches
23.5 × 22.9 cm
Page 73

Vigilance a.k.a. Dust Room, 2023
Mirrors, wood, ducts, fan, extension cords, blue tarp, lights, utility cart, sound, electrical panels, and particles
139 × 235 ¾ × 235 ¾ inches
353.1 × 598.8 × 598.8 cm
Glenstone Museum, Potomac, Maryland
Pages 54–61

David Zwirner and Ebony L. Haynes wish to thank Jane Crawford and Jessamyn Fiore of the Estate of Gordon Matta-Clark and Pope.L, without whom this exhibition and publication would not have been possible. We are deeply appreciative of Greg Lulay for his close collaboration and support. Our thanks are also due to Hamza Walker for participating in an illuminating conversation with Pope.L.

For their work on the exhibition, we are grateful to Rebecca Ashby-Colón, Claire Ball, Susan Cernek, Jenny Cheng, Allison Chipak, Cristina Covucci, Karryl Eugene, Lauren Fisher, Kit Fretz, Richard Gamble, Devon Gilbert, Anne-Claire Giraudon, Daria Harper, Yassel Iglesias, Brandon Israels, Felice Jiang, Jordan Kelly, Coco Kim, Vida Lercari, Francesca Lo Galbo, Julia Lukacher, Alyssa Mattocks, David McBride, Kerry McFate, Mauri Menjivar, Shadi Mirsepassi, Sean Morgan, Clive Murphy, Jena Myung, Haley Parsa, Julian Phillips, Erin Pinover, Nicholas Quint, Kyle Rafferty, Robert Richburg, Antonia Santiago, Gabriela Scopazzi, Virginia Stroh, Natalie Tischler, Lauryn-Ashley Vandyke, Nora Woodin, and Sean Yetter.

Thank you to Andrea Hyde for the catalogue series design and, for their work on this volume, to Bonnie Briant, Sergio Brunelli, Luke Chase, Anna Drozda, Fabio Ferrandini, Zeno Ferrandini, Doro Globus, Elizabeth Gordon, Jessica Palinski Hoos, Amy Hordes, Daniela Ioan, Mari Perina, Molly Stein, Jules Thomson, Joey Young, and Lucas Zwirner.

Pope.L would like to thank 52 Walker principals: Ebony L. Haynes, Gabriela Scopazzi, Sean Morgan, Nora Woodin, and David Zwirner. His gallery: Mitchell-Innes and Nash. Pope.L Studio: Caitlyn Au, Dave Lloyd, and Emily Schultz. The Estate of Gordon Matta-Clark with Jane Crawford and Jessamyn Fiore. And for his interview participation: Hamza Walker.

Also a special thanks to 52 Walker's exhibition team. In addition, Pope.L would like to thank Ravenswood Studios (fabrication): Michael Begora and Michael Shapiro. Morlights (lighting). Mystery Street Recording Company (sound): Geramie Causley and Joe Tessone.

The *Clarion* series is an essential component of 52 Walker programming. An edition accompanies every exhibition, highlighting and expanding on the show's conceptual theses through newly commissioned texts, interviews, archival materials, and artistic interventions. The series is named in honor of the renowned author Octavia E. Butler, who was first published in the 1971 Clarion Science Fiction and Fantasy Writers' Workshop anthology.

Other Titles in the *Clarion* Series
I. Kandis Williams: A Line
II. Nikita Gale: END OF SUBJECT
III. Nora Turato: govern me harder
IV. Tiona Nekkia McClodden: MASK / CONCEAL / CARRY
V. Tau Lewis: Vox Populi, Vox Dei

Forthcoming Titles
VII. Bob Thompson: So let us all be citizens
VIII. Heji Shin: THE BIG NUDES

Published by 52 Walker and
David Zwirner Books
on the occasion of

*Gordon Matta-Clark & Pope.L:
Impossible Failures*
52 Walker, New York
February 3–April 1, 2023

52 Walker
52 Walker Street
New York, New York 10013
+1 212 727 1961
52walker.com

David Zwirner Books
520 West 20th Street, 2nd Floor
New York, New York 10011
+1 212 727 2070
davidzwirnerbooks.com

Editor: Ebony L. Haynes
Project editor: Elizabeth Gordon
Editorial coordinator: Jessica Palinski Hoos
Proofreader: Anna Drozda

Clarion series design: Andrea Hyde
Layout: Bonnie Briant
Photography coordination: Rebecca Ashby-Colón,
    Virginia Stroh
Production manager: Luke Chase
Color separations: VeronaLibri, Verona
Printing: VeronaLibri, Verona

Typefaces: DTL Fleischmann, Genath
Paper: Magno Natural, 140 gsm

Publication © 2024 52 Walker and David Zwirner Books

"Curator's Note: Never a Failed Attempt"
    © 2024 Ebony L. Haynes
"Failin' Good" © 2024 Ebony L. Haynes, Pope.L,
    and Hamza Walker

All artwork and texts by Gordon Matta-Clark © 2023
    Estate of Gordon Matta-Clark/Artists Rights Society
    (ARS), New York

All artwork by Pope.L © 2023 Pope.L

Photography
Unless otherwise noted, all photography is by Kerry McFate.

pp. 13, 14: Courtesy Estate of Gordon Matta-Clark
pp. 31, 32, 33, 34, 35, 37, 38, 39, 41, 98, 99: Stephen Arnold

ISBN 978-1-64423-125-8

Library of Congress Control Number: 2024931137

Printed in Italy

Notes

Notes

Notes